The Cannabis Gourmet Cookbook

Over 120 Delicious Medical Marijuana-Infused Recipes

By Cheri Sicard

The Cannabis Gourmet Cookbook

Published by
Z-Dog Media, LLC
P. O. Box 4914
Long Beach, California 90804
310-827-2299

Library of Congress Control Number: 2011938109
ISBN: 978-0-9839888-0-9

Manufactured in the United States of America
First Printing: 2012

For additional copies of

The Cannabis Gourmet Cookbook

along with marijuana news, politics, and more great recipes,
please visit my Web site, www.CannabisCheri.com.

Dedication

For Joe and Liz Grumbine, two of the kindest, bravest,
and most inspiring people I have ever had the good fortune to know.
I am forever grateful for your friendship.

Acknowledgments

This book would not have been possible without the help and support
of so many people including, but not limited to Sheila Smith Thomas,
Mary Margaret Andrews, Steve Newman, Tanis Westbrook, and the
wonderful folks at Favorite Recipes Press; Mitch Mandell;
Holly Clegg; Sam Sabzehzar; Lanny Swerdlow; Bambi Burnes;
Chuck Burnes; Wanda Smith; Joe Grumbine; Liz Grumbine;
Catrina Coleman; Jeff Spellerberg; Richard Burnes; Tracy Burnes;
and all the amazing members of The Human Solution.

Foreword

As a registered nurse working in a clinic that provides patients with recommendations to use marijuana, the large number of patients who are 55 and older astounds me. When speaking with them about their reasons for wanting to obtain a medical marijuana recommendation, I usually hear the same story:

"Oh, yeah—I used to use marijuana when I was a teen and in my twenties, but I stopped a long time ago."

I always follow up asking, "Why did you stop?"

The answers I get always follow a similar line:

"Oh, I got married," or, "I had kids," or, "I stopped because of my job," or, "I just didn't think I should anymore."

I have never had one person tell me that they stopped using marijuana because it was causing them problems—not one!

Our great grandparents would likely concur. Prior to 1937, cannabis, in one form or another, was found in just about every U.S. medicine cabinet.

Even our ancient ancestors would agree. Five thousand years ago Chinese physicians wrote about their use of cannabis, using it to treat pain, mental health problems, and feminine problems such as menopause and menstrual cramps. Today we use it for these same ailments and a veritable litany of others.

How can one plant provide relief from such a vast array of differing ailments—pain, depression, insomnia, lack of appetite, stress, glaucoma, menopause—the list goes on and on and on? The answer lies in what might be called the active ingredients in marijuana—the cannabinoids.

Due to its psychoactive properties, THC is the cannabinoid that gets all the hype, but it is only one of about 60 cannabinoids found in marijuana. These complex organic molecules have a profound effect on our bodies, if for no other reason than we naturally produce cannabinoids, called endocannabinoids, for a virtual cornucopia of physiological processes. Ingesting marijuana is just supplementing the natural cannabinoids which our body produces and, as such, cannabis should not be seen so much as a medicine but as a supplement.

The term *phytocannabinoids* refers to plants that produce compounds which can activate the body's cannabinoid system. Although cannabis is not the only plant to produce phytocannabinoids, it is the only plant that produces THC, and THC gets all the media coverage.

I don't mean to downplay the importance of THC—it is vitally important to our well being both in terms of everyday health and longevity. It's just that in order to truly understand the importance of ingesting cannabis for maintaining good health, we need to understand the cannabinoid system and the role all the cannabinoids play in that system.

The endocannabinoid system is composed of an ubiquitous number of cannabinoid receptors found in just about every tissue and cell in our bodies, with the most abundant receptors located in the brain. The system works as a biological regulator that maintains homeostasis, a physiological equilibrium resulting from a balance of functions and chemical reactions in our bodies. The two main receptors are the CB1 receptors, located in the brain and on neurons throughout the body; and the CB2 receptors, which are mostly found in the immune system.

Cannabinoids call the shots in basic metabolic processes and govern intercellular communication, especially in the immune and nervous systems. Cannabinoids that we naturally produce (endocannabinoids) along with related compounds (phytocannbinoids) that are found in cannabis interact with our cannabinoid receptors found in tissue, organ, and body systems, modulating and coordinating the functions of the cardiovascular, digestive, endocrine, excretory, immune, musculo-skeletal, nervous, reproductive, and respiratory systems.

The intimate association between our bodies multiple organ systems and the cannabinoid receptors that cover them accounts for the unparalleled ability of cannabis to treat pain, depression, cancers, asthma, wasting syndrome, stress, head injuries, insomnia, and a multitude of other ailments by providing supplemental cannabinoids.

Dr. Robert Melamede, in his seminal publication "Harm Reduction—the Cannabis Paradox," published in the peer-reviewed *Harm Reduction Journal*, proposes that, "The homeostatic action of cannabinoids on so many physiological structures and processes is the basis for the hypothesis that the endocannabinoid system is nothing less than a naturally evolved harm reduction system. Endocannabinoids protect by fine-tuning and regulating dynamic biochemical steady states within the ranges required for healthy biological function."

One of the major ways cannabis works to promote harm reduction is through its action as a potent anti-inflammatory. A powerful example is found in the ability of cannabis to mitigate the effects of autoimmune diseases such as arthritis and multiple sclerosis. By inhibiting the consequences of free-radicals caused by these diseases, cannabis can significantly slow the progression of these debilitating ailments.

Since one of the root causes of the aging process is also the production of excess free-radicals, the cannabinoids found in cannabis can actually slow the aging process itself. I am not saying that cannabis is the fountain of youth—it will not make you young again—but due to its anti-inflammatory properties, the ingestion of supplemental cannabinoids can slow not only the aging process, but also the development of age-related illnesses like cancer, cardiovascular disease, and Alzheimer's disease.

One of the most amazing discoveries about cannabis that has only recently come to light is the anti-cancer properties of this remarkable plant. Dr. Donald Taskhin, in a study conducted for the National Institute of Drug Abuse, found that marijuana smokers are no more likely to develop lung cancer than people who do not smoke marijuana. In fact he actually found evidence that people who smoke marijuana are less likely to develop lung cancer than people who do not smoke marijuana.

In the August 2009 issue of Cancer Prevention Research, seven medical researchers reported that "10 to 20 years of marijuana use was associated with a significantly reduced risk of head and neck squamous cell cancer (HNSCC)."

When the seven researchers used the word significantly in their study, they were not engaging in hyperbole as the study found a 50% or greater reduction of developing this fairly common form of cancer. In other words, it really does the job. It is also important to note that the study indicated that the long term use of cannabis was necessary to achieve this cancer reducing effect—you can't just start ingesting cannabis when you get HNSCC and expect to obtain any significant results. Although short term use after discovery of HNSCC might be beneficial, the prevention of this form of cancer is best obtained when sufficient quantities of cannabis are consumed over the long term.

The anti-cancer properties of cannabinoids are not just limited to HNSCC. In an examination of recently published peer reviewed evidence-based research, medical researchers at the University of Wisconsin School of Medicine and Public Health reported in January 2008 that the administration of cannabinoids halts the spread of a wide range of cancers, including *brain cancer, prostate cancer, breast cancer, lung cancer, skin cancer, pancreatic cancer,* and *lymphomas.* The report also noted that cannabis offers significant advantages over standard chemotherapy treatments because the cannabinoids in cannabis are non-toxic and can uniquely target malignant cells while ignoring healthy ones.

If just half the research showing cannabis can prevent cancer demonstrated that green onions could prevent cancer, there would be legions of doctors and dieticians along with the National Institute of Health, the Surgeon General, and the Federation of Green Onion Growers advising consumption of green onions each day. But because it's marijuana, there is resistance to its medicinal use.

The health of almost all living organisms is dependent on a properly functioning endocannabinoid system. For humans, especially in this day and age of stress, rapidly changing social interactions, and environmental pollution, consumption of supplemental cannabinoids is critical for both the health of the individual and society. Far from being discouraged by oppressive laws and draconian regulations, consumption of cannabis should be encouraged and supported.

Although the medical use of cannabis is absolutely essential, my experience as a Registered Nurse has lead me to conclude that the most beneficial use of cannabis to society is not its medical uses, but its recreational use. It's a simple fact that human beings like to party, and that alteration of one's conscious state is associated with that type of activity. We have done it for so long and so often there is probably a genetic component involved.

Unfortunately the only drug we are officially allowed to use to accomplish this is alcohol, and alcohol is a horrible drug. Prolonged use causes deterioration of heart muscle, cirrhosis of the liver, pancreatitis, and a host of other ailments and injuries that keep our hospitals and morgues filled to overflowing. Alcohol use is the third leading cause of preventable death in the United States, killing some 75,000 Americans each year and shortening their lives by an average of 30 years. Cannabis offers the only viable alternative to facilitating socialization without the problems or horrors associated with the use of alcohol.

The worst calamity to ever befall our country's health in the 20th century was the removal of cannabis from our nation's medicine cabinets. As more states legalize cannabis for medical reasons and millions of Americans re-discover the benefits of cannabis, they are demanding that our government stop lying about the dangers of marijuana and allow it to be available in all its forms safely, reliably, locally, and affordably.

Lanny Swerdlow, RN, LNC
Director, Marijuana Anti-Prohibition Project

Table of Contents

Introduction

Why be a Cannabis Cook?

Cooking with cannabis offers so many benefits, a lot of medical marijuana patients use it as their preferred method of delivering their medicine. Others use "medibles" to regularly augment smoking or vaporizing marijuana. If you've never tried edible marijuana, you might wonder what all the fuss is about, so let's explore some of its advantages:

Smoke Free—One of the things a lot of people like most about edible cannabis is the fact it's completely smoke free. Even though studies like those by UCLA's Dr. Donald Tashkin, MD, find no link between smoking cannabis and cancer (unlike smoking tobacco) and in fact suggest that smoked cannabis might actually prevent cancer[1], a lot of people simply do not like to smoke—period. Others have medical conditions that contraindicate smoking. Edibles to the rescue!

Discreet—Unlike smoking or even vaporizing, edible cannabis provides a discreet way of ingestion. You are the only one who needs to know. Just be sure to eat where nobody is going to ask you to share.

Long Lasting—While the effects of smoked or vaporized marijuana are more immediate, the effects of edible cannabis last longer, 3 to 4 hours or more.

More Effective for Certain Ailments—Certain patients report edible marijuana being a more effective treatment for their conditions. Those who deal with chronic pain, neurological pain, and insomnia might especially benefit from the edible form of THC delivery.

Frugal—If you grow your own marijuana, cooking with cannabis is a thrifty way to use parts of the plant that might otherwise end up in the trash. Leaves and trimmings make fine cannabis-infused butter and oil.

Control—Commercial edibles are usually made from a mixture of different cannabis strains. When you make your own, you can turn the type of cannabis that works best for you into the kinds of foods you like to eat.

The reasons to cook with cannabis are many, but you'll never be able to truly appreciate them until you experience them yourself. So, read the first section of this book to get up to speed, pick out a recipe from the second section, put on your apron, and let's get cooking!

[1] Tashkin, D, et al; Respiratory symptoms and lung function in habitual heavy smokers of marijuana alone, smokers of marijuana and tobacco, smokers of tobacco alone, and nonsmokers. *The American Review of Respiratory Disease*, 1997 Jan;135(1):209-16.

How to Be a Cannabis Cook

Cannabis cooking has come a long way since Alice B. Toklas whipped up batches of her legendary "Haschich Fudge" for Paris's literary elite in the 1920s. While adding pulverized bud to her uncooked concoction might have achieved the desired medicinal result, today's edible marijuana recipes use techniques that make the cuisine every bit as pleasurable as its after-effects. Why struggle with something you need to choke down when the food can be both medicated and delicious?

This chapter will give you the knowledge to become a competent modern cannabis cook. You'll not only understand how edible cannabis works in the body, you'll be able to adapt your own favorite recipes for cannabis cooking and learn about marijuana dosing and unique methods for making infused butter and oils, as well as how to cook with cannabis concentrates. We'll also cover ways to troubleshoot problems typically encountered by homecooks like odor control and unwanted flavors.

Get these basics down, and you'll always be ready to whip up something wonderful in the kitchen whenever and wherever a cannabis cooking opportunity presents itself!

Understanding Edible Marijuana

If your only experience with marijuana has been smoking or vaporizing, cooking with cannabis will open a whole new world to you. Before we explore the differences between inhaled and digested cannabis, let's first look at the most important thing they have in common, Tetrahydrocannabinol or THC.

THC is the chemical component in cannabis that produces the "high" along with many of the plant's medicinal benefits. THC is just one of over 80 cannabinoids isolated in the cannabis plant, and research is ongoing into the medical uses of others. But for our purposes, we are concerned with THC and maintaining its integrity during the cooking process.

In the raw plant, THC is known as THC-A (or THC acid) and is not psychoactive, meaning it won't make you high. It takes aging, heat, or both to make the chemical reaction that converts THC-A to THC occur. This is the primary reason I don't recommend cooking with raw plants (the others being taste and texture) but rather cured, dried marijuana.

While heat activates THC, too much heat—above 392 degrees Fahrenheit—destroys it. Likewise, temperature is always a concern for cannabis cooks (find more details on this on page 24).

You can ingest THC in smoked, vaporized, and edible marijuana, and all of these forms will offer therapeutic benefits, and all will get you high. Now that you know the similarities, let's explore the differences between edible and combustible cannabis.

Metabolism differences— Inhaled marijuana enters the body through the lungs. Edible marijuana is metabolized by the liver, which leads us to the next point.

Speed of onset—When you inhale marijuana, you feel the results almost instantly. When you digest cannabis, it will take at least 30 minutes and as much as an hour and a half or longer before you feel the effects.

Duration of effects—The effects of inhaled cannabis dissipate relatively quickly. An hour or so after smoking, most, if not all, of the effect will have worn off. With edibles, the effects can last for several hours and will usually completely dissipate in about 4 hours.

Dosing challenges—It's easy to get just the right amount of inhaled marijuana. When you feel the effects, you stop. That's the end of it until you smoke more. The strength of edibles can vary widely, even when using similar plant material to make them. Furthermore, because it takes so long to take effect, people often think edibles aren't "working" and eat more, resulting in overmedication (more on dosing and overmedicating on pages 13–16).

Intensity of effects—Edible marijuana is thought to be stronger than smoked or vaporized because of the way it is metabolized through the liver, and also because in the process of combustion or vaporizing some of the THC is burnt off. Since combustion never occurs when making edibles, more THC actually goes into the food.

Conditional effects—Certain medical conditions such as insomnia and chronic pain tend to respond especially well to edible marijuana. For some patients it is not necessary to have a psychoactive dose in order to receive benefit. In fact, for pain management, many patients eat small amounts throughout the day in order to keep a baseline dose in their system without ever feeling high!

Side effects—Regardless of how it is taken, the most commonly reported side effect of using marijuana is what some call "cotton mouth" (dry mouth in medical terms). This unfortunate but not serious side effect tends to be more pronounced with edibles than combustibles.

Why Make Medicated Edibles

Medical marijuana dispensaries are filled with a huge array of enticing edible products, and the list grows longer every day. You may wonder if it's worth the bother to make your own. I say "yes" for several reasons:

When you make it yourself you control the type of marijuana used. Some strains work better for some people than others. If you have a favorite, you can now turn it into an edible form. Most commercial edibles are made from a blend of different plants, and you have no idea what kind of cannabis you are getting. Indica? Sativa? Kush? Swag? Who knows?

When you make it yourself you control the strength. You might be a marijuana lightweight who only needs a small amount to meet your needs. Or you might be someone with a high tolerance who needs twice the amount to be effective. No matter where you are on the spectrum, you can custom dose the edibles you make to meet your specific needs.

You control all the ingredients. Besides cannabis, when you make it yourself you control what you put into your body. Need to cut salt? Want to control fat content? Use only organic ingredients? Make it gluten-free, sugar-free, or vegan? When you make it yourself, the food can be prepared any way you want it.

You can save money. If you grow your own, you almost can't afford not to turn trimmings that would otherwise be discarded into tasty medicated foods (or hash, which can then be turned into tasty medicated foods—See page 20). Even if you don't grow your own medicine, you can often find low-cost trimmings for cooking from someone who does. Ask your provider, and see page 17 for more details.

What Kind of Cannabis to Use

The best kind of marijuana to use in your cooking is the kind that works best for you. Different strains affect people in different ways. A strain that makes one person feel energetic and euphoric might make another person feel anxious or paranoid. The beauty of making your own edibles is that you can customize them for your specific needs.

The number of cannabis strains now available boggles the mind. It will take experimentation with lots of different strains to find the ones that work best for you. Rather than blindly choosing varieties based on their often silly names, a knowledgeable budtender can guide you in the right direction. So can books such as *The Big Book of Buds* series which describe each strain as to its lineage, the type of high you can expect from it, and a detailed color photo so you will physically be able to see if you are getting what is advertised.

While there are far too many individual strains to cover in this book, you should know that there are only three general categories of cannabis. No matter how many cannabis varieties with odd names you see when you visit your provider, all of them can be categorized as an indica, a sativa, or a hybrid.

If you don't know which strain will work well for you, choose by one of these categories.

Think of them as the equivalent of red, white, and rosé in wine, under which there are many varieties.

The descriptions below are general statements, and you should evaluate how each type of cannabis effects you personally. Most people switch between the types at different times and for different purposes.

Indica—Indica strains are known for giving a "body high." Their effects tend to be relaxing and felt throughout the entire body. Indicas are especially good at bedtime.

Sativa—Sativa strains are known for giving a "head high." Their effect tends to be more energizing. Many people like sativas for sparking creativity. If you need to be awake and alert while using medication, a sativa is usually the right choice.

Hybrids—Hybrids are, of course, a mix of the two. This has benefits as sometimes the dominant quality of a pure indica or a pure sativa is too much. For instance, some people just get too sleepy with a pure indica. Others feel anxiety or paranoia with a pure sativa. A hybrid can mitigate the negatives and accentuate the positives. Depending on the strain, it may be indica or sativa dominant. Check with your doctor, budtender, or reference books for recommendations that may work well for you.

Of course, there's no requirement for you to be such a connoisseur. You don't have to cook with just one kind of cannabis. Most commercially produced cannabis edibles contain a mixture of different plants and strains, and you can do the same as well. The edibles you make are your creations, and you can make them with whatever material works for you in whatever combinations you need. Continue reading to learn how.

Edible Marijuana Essentials

Both combustible and edible marijuana depend on THC to produce the "high."

The effects of edible marijuana have a longer onset and take longer to dissipate than combustible cannabis.

The most common marijuana side effect is dry mouth, and this effect tends to be more pronounced with edible marijuana.

It is not necessary to feel high in order to experience medicinal benefits from marijuana.

Indica strains tend to produce a relaxing "full body high."

Sativa strains tend to produce energetic, creative "head highs."

Hybrid strains combine the best of indicas and sativas in varying proportions.

Calculating Cannabis Cooking Dosages

It is impossible for any recipe writer to make an across-the-board recommendation for the amount of cannabis a given dish needs to be effective. Far too many variables come into play. By nature cannabis recipes, including the ones in this book, must include an amount of marijuana to use. But it is important for the cook to always understand that these amounts are only recommendations that are to be used as a rough guideline.

When you inhale cannabis, either via smoking or vaporizing, you feel the effects almost instantly. It's easy to get a proper dose. When you've had enough, you simply stop. The effects will wear off relatively quickly as well. Getting the perfect dose with edible marijuana is trickier.

Unless you're lucky enough to have access to a lab that tests your medicine for potency, dosing is where cooking with cannabis becomes art more than science. While some dispensaries do offer testing services, at this point they are few and far between, and are cost prohibitive when available. I actually had a testing lab rep suggest that I needed to have the recipes in this book tested. She then went on to explain that to be totally accurate, each one would probably need 3 separate tests (I'm not sure why). The price came to nearly $1,000. Per recipe!

Don't worry. People have been managing to successfully dose their cannabis edibles for thousands of years without the benefit of testing labs. With care, experimentation, and the tips and techniques contained in this chapter, you will get the knack of knowing how much cannabis to use in your cooking.

Dosing Considerations

Before we get into the process of determining exactly how much marijuana to use in our cooking, there are some important key points that need to be understood.

All cannabis is not created equal! The same amounts of different strains of marijuana will NOT be equal in potency. Identical strains from different growers or even different crops of the same strain, from the same grower, will vary. Just because you have cooked with a given strain in the past does not mean that you will know the strength of the food made from the same strain from a different source. Testing laboratories show wide ranges in potency within the same strain, depending on where and how it was grown. Even home growers who use the same techniques and nutrients, and start with clones from the same mother plant, may expect some variations from crop to crop.

Aside from potency, every cannabis strain is different, each containing varying degrees of specific cannabinoids. This is why some strains make you sleepy while others make you energetic. If you are cooking with a new strain, test its potency and effects both before cooking and before eating a normal portion (see page 14) in order to estimate its strength.

Even though there may be some variations, keeping notes on the strains you cook with has real value. As you become more experienced and try different marijuana strains in edibles, you will find some work better for you than others. Carefully evaluate how you feel after trying each new strain. Does it make you sleepy? Energetic? Euphoric? Paranoid or anxious? Any of these effects can be achieved or mitigated by experimenting with different strains. A knowledgeable budtender can be your best friend in choosing new strains to try. You can expect similar results when using the same strain in the future, even though the strength of the new plant may or may not be the same.

In addition to the type and quality of the marijuana used in cooking, other variables will affect the strength of the edibles involved:

The weight of the person eating the food will alter how much they feel the medication. Naturally, larger people usually need larger doses and smaller people, smaller doses. I say usually, because again, different individuals have different metabolisms and tolerance levels and likewise react to cannabis in different ways.

The frequency the person uses cannabis will affect how much they will need to physically feel the effects. The more you use, the greater your tolerance will tend to be. However, frequent and heavy cannabis consumers who stop for even a day or two will likely experience a heightened effect the first time they use marijuana again after abstaining.

Eating marijuana edibles on an empty stomach will cause you to feel their effect more quickly and profoundly than if you had consumed them after eating other foods or in conjunction with other foods.

Before adding cannabis to your cooking, consider the desired final outcome. Some patients want little, if any, psychotropic effect. Others seek a strong high. Dose accordingly.

Alcohol can compound the effects of cannabis, and for many people the mix of alcohol and cannabis produces an unpleasant paranoid effect. Reduce, or better yet eliminate, alcohol consumption when using marijuana.

Recommended Dosage Ranges

Some medical conditions do not require a psychotropic dose of cannabis to obtain the desired results. Many patients are able to control their conditions by eating tiny amounts of medicated foods throughout the day. While they never feel "high," they do get medicinal benefits such as pain relief, inflammation control, and appetite stimulation. Others require and/or desire stronger doses.

The following chart will give a dose range for using leaf/trim, bud, and concentrates. There is a large range, as you can see. This is because each strain is different, containing a different mix of cannabinoids in varying strengths. The dosage range for concentrates is even wider.

I will stress again that the information below is a very general guideline that needs to be weighed against the factors covered above when determining the amount of cannabis to use in your recipes. The amounts are suggested for a person of about 150 pounds. Try to determine an amount that seems reasonable for your needs, taking into account the strength of the plant material used and the factors listed above. When you've finished cooking, use the testing techniques described on page 15 to assess your dosing skills and adjust the edible's portion size accordingly.

Cannabis Material	Recommended Dosage Range Per Individual Dose
Marijuana Leaf/Trim	1/2 to 2 grams
Average Bud	1/4 to 1 gram
High Quality Bud	1/8 to 1/2 gram
Kief or Hash	1/8 to 2 grams

What if the Dose is Too High?

Getting too strong a dose is a common problem, especially with people who are new to using edible marijuana. In fact, there is no easier way to get too much marijuana than by eating it and no quicker way to get turned off to edibles than by ingesting too much cannabis. Because it can take an hour and a half or more for the medicine to take effect (two to three hours if you didn't take it on an empty stomach), some people think it's not working and eat more. By the time it all kicks in they realize they've overdone it.

If this happens to you or someone you know, first and foremost, do not panic! It is impossible to ingest a toxic dose of marijuana. Don't take my word for it. Here's what the World Health Organization had to say on the subject.

"There are no recorded cases of overdose fatalities attributed to cannabis, and the estimated lethal dose for humans extrapolated from animal studies is so high that it cannot be achieved by users[1]."

So overdosing on marijuana will not kill you. It just does not work that way in the body. It does not slow your respiratory system or cause organ failure even in extreme doses. So calm down. You don't need to worry about those things.

That said, it is definitely possible to ingest more marijuana than you need or want. When this happens, you may have feelings of uneasiness, anxiety, or even paranoia. You might also feel dizzy, groggy, nauseous, or get chills. Your coordination might be affected, and likewise you may have trouble talking clearly and could lose your balance when walking. Some people experience heart rate acceleration, which can further increase the anxiety.

It goes without saying you should not be driving or operating heavy machinery. The most common real danger in overmedicating comes in the form of falls or accidents related to impairment of motor skills. Likewise you should especially exercise caution and consult your cannabis physician if you have a medical condition that already causes any of the symptoms listed above. You wouldn't want to dismiss serious signals your body is sending because you attributed them to overmedicating on marijuana.

The best remedy for ingesting too much cannabis is to simply sleep it off. The peak of the effects should take place about an hour after you begin to notice them and then begin to dissipate after that. It's common to feel anxious or hyperactive in the first hour, before becoming tired afterwards. Lie down, go to sleep, and when you wake up a few hours later it will all be over. Unlike indulging in too much alcohol, you won't even have to deal with a hangover.

Should you discover a given batch of any recipe is stronger than you want it to be, don't discard it! The remedy is simple: consume a smaller portion in order to decrease the dosage.

How to Test an Edible's Strength

A quick way to get an indication of the strength of the cannabis *before* cooking with it is to smoke or vaporize a small amount. While cooking will produce a somewhat different and often stronger effect, smoking or vaporizing will give you a ballpark idea of what to expect in regard to potency.

If you don't know how strong a given batch of cannabis butter, oil, or edibles is, and you usually won't, it's best to test the waters before chowing down with gusto. Start with a half portion, or even a quarter portion if you consider yourself a "lightweight." Wait at least an hour and a half. If you feel the effects of the marijuana, don't eat any more. If you don't, try another piece, or alternatively, wait until the next day and try a larger portion. Even if you don't feel a "high" you will still be getting medicinal benefits.

---

1. Hall, W, et al; WHO Project on Health Implications of Cannabis Use, A Comparative Appraisal of the Health and Psychological Consequences of Alcohol, Cannabis, Nicotine, and Opiate Use, 1995 Aug.

Dosing Essentials

When determining dosing, be sure to consider the weight and tolerance level of the user in addition to the strength and strain of the marijuana.

The potency of the same marijuana strain will vary from grower to grower and even crop to crop.

While eating too much marijuana might result in an unpleasant experience, it is not dangerous or fatal and will pass in 4 to 8 hours.

Keep marijuana edibles well labeled in order to avoid confusion with regular foods, and keep them out of reach of those not allowed access.

Making and Using Cannabis-Infused Butter and Oil

Since THC, the psychoactive component of marijuana, is fat soluble, butter and oil make ideal ways to bond the cannabinoids to food. Likewise, cannabis-infused butter, margarine, or cooking oils are the backbone of many medicated foods. With these staples stored in your refrigerator or freezer, you're always ready for a cannabis cooking opportunity whenever the need or mood strikes.

You can cook with any kind of marijuana from trimmings to flowers, and, as discussed on pages 13–15, you will need to adjust the amount used depending on the potency of the plant and what parts of it you are using.

I've listed the amounts I used to test the recipes in this book below. You can and should alter the suggested amounts to meet your needs, but these will give you a starting guideline. To make about 1 cup you will need the following:

For Canna-Butter or Margarine

1 1/4 cups unsalted butter or margarine
1 ounce average to high quality trim or low quality dried bud,
    or 1/2 ounce average quality dried bud
About 4 cups water

For Canna-Oil

1 1/4 cups cooking oil: olive, vegetable, canola, corn, peanut,
    or grapeseed. (You can even infuse solid-at-room-temperature
    fats like coconut oil or vegetable shortening should you choose.)
1 ounce average to high quality trim or low quality dried bud,
    or 1/2 ounce average quality dried bud
About 4 cups water

You can use more than the recommended amount of cannabis in order to make your butter or oil more concentrated. This has advantages, especially if you are trying to lose weight or cut calories, as the more potent and concentrated your butter or oil, the less of it you'll need to use to achieve a proper dose. On the downside, the more concentrated the fat, the stronger its herbal flavor and green color.

The recipes that use cannabis-infused oil in this book call for either olive oil, because of its specific flavor profile, or neutral oil, because of its lack thereof. Neutral oils include vegetable oil, canola oil, or grapeseed oil and, to a lesser extent, corn and peanut oils (which can sometimes have a strong flavor, sometimes not). You can freely swap out neutral oils in recipes with no quality compromise. In a pinch you can even use olive oil for neutral oil, albeit with a little added flavor; conversely, swapping neutral oils for olive oil in a recipe will also work technically, just with a little less flavor complexity. Since you will never cook cannabis-infused oil at high temperatures, smoke point levels pose no concern for cannabis cooks.

Cannabis for Cooking

You will want to cook with cured dried marijuana, not fresh green plants. (While new research is emerging on the health benefits of consuming raw cannabis, it's far outside the scope of this book.) Prepare plant material by making sure all large stems and stalks are removed. Aside from this there is no need to grind the plant material, despite the recommendations of many internet sites. In fact, grinding makes it more difficult to remove later.

More expensive plant material does not necessarily mean better cooking material. There's a saying in the marijuana industry, "smell sells," referring to the fact that consumers tend to favor tight pretty buds with a pungent aroma. The savvy cannabis consumer should also know that testing laboratories have found these qualities to be no indication as to a product's potency. While nice-smelling marijuana might provide a more enjoyable smoke, there is no reason for the cannabis cook to pay for this "benefit" as it will only be wasted in the process of creating edibles.

If you find you have more dried plant material than you can cook with right away, store it in a well sealed plastic bag in the freezer until you're ready. The cold temperature prevents the growth of molds and also helps retain the marijuana's potency over time.

Why Water?

You might be wondering why I include water as an ingredient. Including water, especially when cooking on the stovetop, ensures the cannabis will never reach a higher temperature than the boiling point or 212 degrees F. More importantly, the chlorophyll and terpenes—the parts of the plant that give it its flavor and color—are water soluble, and most will likewise bind to water during the cooking process instead of infusing themselves into the fats along with the THC. In practical terms this means less herbal flavor and green color in the finished marijuana-infused butter or oil.

That said, the butter or oil might still appear mighty green, even when cooked with water. The amount will vary from strain to strain with some coming out pale green or almost yellow, while others take on a deep forest green color. Keep in mind, however, that color has nothing to do with potency.

Without water in the mix, the plant material absorbs too much of the butter and oil. This means that usable product is going into the trash, a problem that's reduced when adding water. The increased liquid volume also gives cooks the option to add more plant material in order to make more concentrated infusions if they wish.

Most instructions you find on the internet for making butter advise cooking the butter with water, but most oil making instructions do not. I've never understood why not. The same principles apply. It takes a little extra work to separate oil from the water afterwards, but your effort will be well rewarded with a better, more mild flavored finished product.

Cooking Methods

You can cook cannabis butter or oil on the stovetop or in a slow cooker. Of the two, I strongly prefer the slow cooker method and suggest that if you plan on cooking with cannabis with any regularity, it's well worth picking up a large slow cooker. This inexpensive kitchen appliance, which you can also use to make convenient nonmedicated meals, offers several advantages over the stovetop method:

Allows you to start cooking and forget about it for hours without having to monitor temperature or water levels.

Allows infusion to occur slowly at a consistent low temperature over a long period of time.

Reduces the amount of odor over stovetop cooking.

Hamilton Beach makes a line of slow cookers called "Stay and Go" that seal and clamp closed in order to make it easy for cooks to transport foods to potluck dinners and parties. While the cannabis cook doesn't necessarily need the clamp function when making butter and oil, the rubber gasket seal on the lid is useful as it seals almost all the odor inside the crock. Unless you open the lid, there is hardly any smell at all. It works so well that I made a batch of marijuana butter in a "Stay and Go" slow cooker while having a business meeting in the adjoining room. Nobody had a clue until I told them. I don't get paid to endorse this product (in fact I have no idea how the Hamilton Beach company would feel about being recommended in a marijuana cookbook). I just know that it works!

How to Make Cannabis-Infused Butter or Oil

Slow Cooker Method: Add butter or oil, plant material, and water to the slow cooker and cook on low for 8 to 16 hours. I know some cooks who cook their butter for as much as 2 or 3 days in the slow cooker. Feel free to do so if you choose. It seems like overkill to me and after having tested longer cooking times, I found no improvement in quality or potency. In fact, I noticed a stronger herbal flavor and not much else.

Or

Stovetop Method: Place butter or oil, plant material, and water in a large lidded Dutch oven on the stovetop. Bring to a boil, reduce heat to very low, and simmer for 6 to 12 hours. Take care to monitor the liquid level often, adding water as necessary to always keep at least 3 cups in the pot. Simmering marijuana on the stovetop is very aromatic. If you're worried about nosy neighbors, cook other strong-smelling foods such as roasting garlic at the same time in order to help camouflage the smell. Better still, use a slow cooker.

Drain, Rinse, Strain

The method of draining is the same for stovetop and slow cooker methods. Place a cheesecloth-lined strainer over a large pot or bowl, and strain the liquid through this. Before discarding plant material, pour a large kettle full of boiling water over the full strainer in order to wash through any extra butter or oil clinging to the plant material. Allow to cool then squeeze out as much liquid as possible. Discard the plant material. Now chill the rest, water and oil or liquid butter. The fats will rise to the top.

Butter will harden into a solid when chilled, making it easy for you to simply lift the piece off of the water below and discard the water. Rinse the butter chunk with cold, fresh water to wash off any of the canna-water or plant material left on the butter.

Oil will rise to the top of the water but often won't solidify. No problem. You can use a spoon to skim the oil off the water. Even better is a kitchen gadget called a gravy separator, which looks like a small pitcher with the spout originating on the bottom. This unique design allows the water to be poured out while retaining every drop of the oil floating at the top. During the Thanksgiving and Christmas holidays, gravy separators are sold everywhere; otherwise, find them at gourmet shops. You can also find extra-large gravy separators year-round at restaurant supply stores.

Now it's time to strain one more time to remove as much sediment as possible. Place a double layer of cheesecloth over a strainer and pour the oil mixture through. To strain butter, melt it, strain, then chill again until solid.

Refrigerate infused butter or oil until ready to use, or freeze for even longer storage. Fats can still go rancid in the freezer so try to use within 3 months.

You're now ready to start cooking with canna-butter and canna-oil!

Butter and Oil Essentials

Cook with dried cured plant material, not raw plants.

Making butter or oil in a slow cooker offers several advantages over the stovetop method.

Cooking butter and oil with water improves flavor and prevents burning.

Straining a second time removes most sediment.

Refrigerate infused butter or oil, or freeze for longer storage.

Cooking with Concentrates

Cooking with concentrates opens up a whole new world of recipes that can be converted to cannabis cooking. A lot of these recipes contain far less fat than ones that depend on butter or oil to carry the medication, an important consideration for those trying to curb calories or limit fats. Of course cannabis metabolizes better with some fat, but when you cook with concentrates, you eliminate the need to add extra oil or butter to achieve a proper dose.

When cooking for my own use, as opposed to developing recipes for others, I almost always use hash. I find that its slightly nutty flavor naturally blends in better with more foods than the herbal undertones contained in marijuana-infused butter and oil.

Before we go further, let's define the terms so everyone is on the same page:

Kief is a powdery substance composed of the resinous glands or trichomes on the marijuana plant. The powder can range from somewhat sticky to gummy depending on the plant and strain.

Hash is kief that has been heated and pressed. Hash can range from gold to dark green or brown in color and from a dry, crumbly, powdery texture all the way to a sticky, putty-like substance, and all points in between.

Hash and kief are known as cannabis concentrates because they contain the part of the plant that contains the THC, without much of anything else. In practical terms, this means far less herbal flavor in the finished food. The potency of a given concentrate, of course, depends on the quality of the plant that dedicated its glands to making it.

Hash and kief can be used interchangeably in recipes. Specific dosing ranges can be found on page 14.

Legal Heads Up!

Be aware that concentrates like kief and hash are in more of a legal limbo than regular marijuana in some areas of the country and carry harsher consequences and penalties in others. In some states being arrested with hash will earn you some serious felony charges—up to a life sentence in Oklahoma (in the year 2011 in the so-called "land of the free and home of the brave").

Even some of the states that do allow medical marijuana for qualified patients do not allow kief or hash. Still other states that don't specifically prohibit concentrates have cities or counties within them that do. None of it makes any sense. After all, kief and hash are the exact same herb as marijuana, just without the plant material, but laws are laws until we do something to change them. Check your local ordinances in order to stay legal, compliant, and as safe as possible in the complicated, confusing, and ever-evolving world of marijuana and the law.

Kief Happens

If you are lucky enough to have a medical marijuana purveyor who offers hash or kief, you have an easy way to access this potent cooking ingredient. But depending how much you use and/or handle cannabis, kief may be happening all around you everyday.

Many of the handheld grinders marijuana smokers regularly use come with built in kief screens. It might take a while to build enough kief to cook with, but every little bit helps, so always save it.

A lot of people use small electric coffee grinders to prepare their medicine for smoking or vaporizing. Kief accumulates on the inside lid and bowl of these devices fairly quickly as a side effect of their grinding job. Once you notice a thick, sticky film coating the grinder, unplug it, take a dull knife, and start carefully scraping it out. This is kief, and once you have enough of it, it is excellent to use in cooking.

You can also purchase or make small kief screening boxes (the internet is full of how-to instructions). The boxes contain an ultra-fine mesh screen that is used as a sieve. The dried marijuana bud goes in and is shaken over the screen. The plant material stays on top but the tiny resinous glands drop through the finely woven mesh. You can still smoke or vaporize the bud that's left, but it will be significantly less potent. For those who process large amounts of cannabis, there are commercial products available that make kief collection easy and time efficient.

If you grow even small amounts of your own marijuana, or help someone who does, you will find what is known as "scissor hash" accumulating on your trimming tools. Since it hasn't been pressed or heated, it isn't technically "hash," but it is sticky kief. Every now and then while trimming the harvest, use a knife or razor blade to carefully scrape off the sticky resin and roll it into a ball.

You will notice the same substance accumulating on your fingers (or on your gloves if you wear them for trimming). This is known as, you guessed it, "finger hash." If you are using bare hands, every now and then roll the hash off your fingers and start accumulating a ball that you can add to as necessary. If you wear latex gloves for trimming, allow the finger hash to accumulate, then place the gloves in the freezer for a few hours as the cold will make it easier to remove the finger hash from the gloves. Simply rub the still frozen gloves vigorously over a collection receptacle (a large piece of paper works well), and the cold kief will fall like snow.

It's a good idea to always trim over a tray or plastic mat, as powdery kief will fall as you are working with the plant. At the end of the day, pile it all up and save it for cooking.

If you are growing your own medicine, you will probably want to make your own hash. Hash making is outside the scope of this book, but know that it will take about a $100 investment in tools and a little time. Making hash isn't difficult, and you will be well rewarded with first-rate cooking (and smoking) material for your efforts.

Quick & Easy Marijuana Butter or Oil

If you don't have any cannabis-infused butter or oil on hand, you can make some up quickly using kief or hash. The amount of concentrates you will need to use will vary depending on quality (refer to pages 13–15), but the process of making butter or oil with hash or kief is fuss free and far less messy and aromatic than using leaf or bud. Simply melt the butter or heat oil over low heat. Stir in hash or kief until dissolved. Your butter or oil is now ready to use in recipes.

How to Cook with Kief or Hash

As we discussed earlier, kief and hash can range from dry and crumbly to sticky and gummy. Most smokers prefer the latter, but for cooking purposes, the dry, crumbly, powdery stuff is often easiest to work with. Good news—it's usually less expensive too.

Dry hash is easier to work with because it is easy to grind, which then allows you to stir the fine powder into all kinds of foods, something impossible to do with the gummy type of hash. If you plan on dissolving the hash in a hot liquid, however, either type will work fine. Once dissolved the kief or hash is easy to evenly incorporate into the food. In some delicate foods, the concentrates might add a very slight gritty texture, just barely enough to let you know it's there. In other dishes the hash or kief completely disappears into the texture of the food.

Like any cannabis edible, your hash or kief-infused food needs some fat to help it metabolize effectively. If you do want to add hash or kief to a fat-free food, be sure to accompany the food with another dish that does contain some fat, or wash it down a glass of milk, or coffee or tea with cream, or some other fat-containing beverage.

The other consideration when cooking with any kind of cannabis is temperature. Remember that THC evaporates at temperatures greater than 392 degrees F. You can cook at temperatures higher than that, as long as the temperature of the food itself doesn't get that high. For more details on cannabis cooking temperatures, refer to page 24–26.

Depending on the recipe, add hash or kief to cooking in these ways:

If your recipe involves any heated liquids, dissolve the hash or kief in the liquid before proceeding.

When adding to long-cooking liquids, such as soups and stews, stir in the concentrate to dissolve about 5 minutes before serving.

Beat finely crumbled kief or hash into fat-containing ingredients before incorporating into the recipe. This works well for foods like mayonnaise, sour cream, cream cheese, yogurt, butter, oil, milk, beaten eggs, etc.

Substitute hash or kief for bud or leaf when making cannabis-infused butter or oils.

Cooking with Tinctures

Tinctures are cannabis concentrates made by steeping marijuana in alcohol or glycerin. Tinctures are designed to be taken sublingually, in other words, under the tongue. When taken this way, they take effect quickly, not as quickly as smoking, but almost.

I have seen a lot of recipes out there using marijuana tincture as a method of delivering the medicine in the food. You won't find any in this book. I personally don't like to cook with tinctures for several reasons.

While the THC in cannabis can be activated with alcohol or glycerin, it isn't as effective as doing so with fats, meaning some potency is lost.

Sublingual ingestion of tinctures just seems to work more effectively than digestion.

It takes A LOT of plant material to make a good tincture. If I am going to go to that much trouble and expense, I want to use it in the most effective way.

But that's just me. You may discover you like cooking with tinctures. If so, it's easy to do. Just add a few drops—whatever dose you would normally use—to whatever food you are eating.

Concentrates Essentials

Kief is composed of the resinous glands or trichomes from the cannabis plant.

Hash is kief that has been heated and pressed.

You can make cannabis oil or butter by using hash or kief instead of leaf or bud.

You can forego making cannabis butter or oil and simply add finely ground kief or hash to the recipe instead.

Since most of the chlorophyll and other plant materials have been removed, cooking with hash or kief will impart far less herbal flavor to the finished dish.

Tinctures are concentrated marijuana infusions made with alcohol or glycerin.

Adapting Your Favorite Recipes for Cannabis Cooking

I've provided lots of tasty, tested cannabis recipes in this book. The internet is filled with others, some good, some not. But I bet you already have favorite recipes in your cooking repertoire you want to make with cannabis. Many recipes adapt easily to cannabis cooking. Let's explore how to do it.

Cooking and Use Considerations

Remember THC evaporates at temperatures greater than 392 degrees F. You can cook at temperatures higher than that, as long as the temperature of the food itself doesn't get that high (no pun intended).

Baked foods pose no problems when cooking with cannabis even at oven temperatures in excess of 400 degrees F. The same can be said of foods that are deep-fried, as long as the internal temperature of the food itself doesn't go above 392 degrees F, and the cannabis is contained inside the food. If you put the cannabis in the batter or breading, on the other hand, you've probably wasted some good marijuana.

You also have to be careful when sautéing, as the surface temperatures of foods can get very high. Depending on the recipe, you may be able to sauté, providing the cannabis is contained inside the food and the internal temperature doesn't get too high. You always want to avoid using cannabis butter or oil as the fat that goes into the pan. Rather use them as the fats that go into the food.

I recently attended a marijuana cooking class in which the chef/instructor touted the use of cannabis-infused oil in marinades. I was incredulous. Sure you could swap canna-oil for regular in marinades, but why in the world would you want to? While a tiny amount of the oil in marinades will be absorbed into the food, most of it will end up in the trash. For most people, cannabis is an expensive cooking ingredient. Don't waste it in a marinade. Add it to the food that will actually be consumed instead.

Metabolic Considerations

In order for the THC in cannabis to metabolize, it needs the presence of fat, alcohol, or glycerin. For our purposes, we need to consider the fat content of foods. If you are cooking with marijuana-infused butter or oil, this step is covered. But when cooking with kief or hash, keep in mind that the recipe needs to contain some fat. This can come in the form of butter or oil, but it doesn't have to. Eggs, cream, whole milk, yogurt, cheeses, meats, tofu, avocados, nuts, and all kinds of other foods contain fat. Any of them will work to help activate the THC in your recipe. Dairy products work especially well in cannabis cooking because of the presence of lecithin, an emulsifier that helps bind THC to fat. Vegetarian and vegans should note that lecithin is also present in many milk substitutes, including soy milk and rice milk. You could medicate a fat-free food with hash or kief as well, providing you consume it along with another food or drink that contains fat.

Flavor Considerations

Generally speaking, the more delicate the recipe's flavors, the harder it will be to make it taste good with cannabis added. Unless you enjoy the herbal flavor of marijuana infusing your foods, and some people do, you will want to consider the flavor profile of the recipe you are trying to adapt.

I'm not saying you will eliminate all traces of marijuana flavor, nor should you try to. I have sampled plenty of medicated foods that had no medicated flavor, but not one of them had any noticeable effect on me either. If you don't like feeling high, this may be OK. Remember, you do not need to physically feel high in order to receive medicinal benefits. But let's be honest. Most people do want to feel something from their medibles. For that to happen, you will usually have some discernible flavor of cannabis in the food, unless you have a very low threshold or a highly spiced food, or both!

There are, however, things you can do to reduce the amount of "green" flavor in your foods. The most important step begins when you make infused butter or oil—see page 16–19 for details.

Once you have canna-butter or oil, or even when preparing foods with kief and hash, cannabis cooking is not the time for daintily seasoned foods. Use a heavy hand with herbs, spices, seasonings, and intensely flavored ingredients as these can help mask unwanted herbal flavors. Look for dishes that have a lot going on flavor wise and that use a lot of different ingredients, for example pizza with the works, and you just might be able to lose all of the unwanted taste while maintaining potency.

Dosing Considerations

Creative cannabis cooks always need to keep dosing in mind in order to make sure their recipes carry the right amount of cannabis to give a proper per-serving dose. Likewise, it's important to know the yield of an entire recipe as well as how many servings that constitutes before adding medicine in order to know how much marijuana to use. Multiply the number of servings by the amount of each dose and cook accordingly. For instance, if you are making a recipe designed for 6 servings and using 1/2 gram per serving the amount would be 6 times 1/2 gram, or 3 grams total for the recipe.

When cooking with cannabis-infused oil or butter you can always add kief or hash to augment the recipe if there is not enough butter or oil for dosing. Conversely, if a recipe uses more butter or oil than you need to deliver a proper dose, substitute regular butter or oil to make up the difference.

Cooking with Bud

Can you forgo making infused butter or oil and simply stir ground bud into your foods? Sure you can, but more often than not you shouldn't. This is because of the less-than-appetizing flavor and texture that can result. There are a few exceptions when cooking with dried cannabis flowers that work well, provided the buds are finely ground. Meatballs and ground meat mixtures, especially those containing lots of other seasonings and ingredients, make good vehicles for ground bud. You can also get away with it by adding as you would any other herb near the end of cooking, in strongly flavored sauces such as Italian-style tomato sauces, or Mexican-style cooked chile salsas.

Recipe Adapting Essentials

Make sure the cooking method keeps the internal food temperature below 392 degrees F.

Make sure the recipe contains some fat to help metabolize the THC.

Use a heavy hand with seasonings and strongly flavored ingredients in recipes to help counter unwanted herbal flavors.

Add cannabis to the actual food, not the marinade or breading.

Search for recipes that have high oil or butter content.

Recipes with lots of different flavors going on usually work well.

Know the yield and serving sizes of a recipe in order to calculate the proper amount of cannabis to add.

The Recipes

The recipes in this book are tasty enough to use even when you don't want to medicate (or for friends and family members who abstain from marijuana)—just leave out the cannabis.

Whenever possible I have included instructions for freezing and reheating recipes. Cannabis cooking is expensive, and there's no need to waste it just because you don't need the whole amount a recipe makes at once.

Pay attention to the number of servings and serving sizes for each recipe in order to monitor the amount of marijuana you are ingesting and/or serving. Where possible I have written the recipes to make portioning easy, as in cupcakes or tarts instead of whole cakes or pies, but other recipes will take willpower.

About the Dosages in the Recipes

When it comes to the recommended amount of cannabis to use in the recipes in this book, know they are calculated for an experienced regular user of edible marijuana. If you are new to edibles or consider yourself a "lightweight," you will definitely want to use less marijuana when making butter or oil and less hash or kief in recipes calling for those. Always err on the side of caution, and carefully test your edibles before indulging in too much. Most recipes calling for oil or butter will give a dose of about 1/2 gram person (if you use my recipes for making butter or oil). Recipes for kief and hash will give about 1/4 gram per person. Scale up or down as your individual needs dictate.

Always Label and Protect

It is the duty of any responsible cannabis cook to make sure that marijuana edibles stay out of the wrong hands, or don't accidentally get into the hands of someone who doesn't know what they are ingesting. Always label foods well to avoid confusion, especially those in the freezer, and keep cannabis edibles segregated and safely out of reach of those who are not allowed access.

Snacks & Appetizers

A light snack or premeal appetizer is a great way to medicate with food. Cannabis edibles are more effective on an empty stomach. Foods like spreads, dips, and small bites also make it easy to take in just a little bit, which is especially helpful for patients managing pain with cannabis edibles who need to keep a small but consistent amount in their systems throughout the day.

Look in your own recipe collection and you are sure to come up with more ways to add cannabis to snacks and appetizers. The aforementioned dips and spreads are natural candidates, as are the indulgent hors d'oeuvres recipes that magazines feature each holiday season.

Guacamole Deluxe

In order to evenly distribute the cannabis in the avocado, mash this dip a bit more than you might when making a non-medicated guacamole. Serve as a dip with chips or as an addition to tacos, burritos or quesadillas.

Yield: About 1 1/2 cups/6 servings   Serving Size: 1/4 cup

2 medium ripe avocados
1 1/2 grams kief or finely ground dry hash
1 medium ripe tomato
1/4 cup finely chopped red or yellow onion
1 small green onion, finely chopped
1/4 teaspoon minced garlic

1 medium jalapeño pepper, cored, seeded and minced
2 tablespoons finely chopped cilantro
1 tablespoon lime juice
Salt and pepper to taste

Place peeled, pitted avocados in the bowl of a food processor. Sprinkle kief or hash over the surface of the avocados and pulse 15 to 20 times or until avocado is coarsely chopped and cannabis is more or less evenly distributed. Add remaining ingredients and continue to pulse the food processor until ingredients are evenly combined and texture is almost smooth.

Sun-Dried Tomato Tapenade

Like Black Olive Tapenade (page 29), use this colorful spread on baguette slices for appetizers or as a sandwich spread or pasta or pizza topping.

Yield: 1/2 cup/8 servings   Serving Size: 1 tablespoon

1/2 (10- to 12-ounce) jar oil-packed sun-dried tomatoes, drained, reserve oil
1 large garlic clove, peeled
2 grams kief or finely ground hash

Salt and pepper to taste
2 tablespoons olive oil reserved from sun-dried tomato jar

Place all ingredients except olive oil in a food processor or blender and purée. Slowly pour in olive oil with machine running to blend. Chill until ready for use.

Freezer Friendly!
Place extra black olive or sun-dried tomato tapenade in a lidded freezer container and freeze. Thaw in refrigerator or bring to room temperature to use.

Black Olive Tapenade

Add a thin layer of this intensely flavorful spread to a toasted baguette slice, with or without a smear of goat cheese or cream cheese, and you have an instant snack. You can also use this versatile tapenade as a sandwich spread or pasta or pizza topping.

Yield: 1/2 cup/8 servings   Serving Size: 1 tablespoon

1/2 cup pitted kalamata olives
2 large garlic cloves, peeled
1 teaspoon drained capers
2 teaspoons lemon juice
1/2 teaspoon minced fresh rosemary, or
   1/4 teaspoon dried

1/2 teaspoon minced fresh thyme, or
   1/4 teaspoon dried
2 grams kief or finely ground hash
Salt and pepper to taste
1 tablespoon olive oil

Place all ingredients except olive oil in a food processor or blender and purée. Slowly pour in olive oil with machine running to blend. Chill until ready for use.

Hot Artichoke Dip

The unique flavor of artichokes blends beautifully with cream cheese in this classic warm party dip. Serve with crusty bread.

Yield: 2 1/4 cups/9 servings   Serving Size: 1/4 cup

1 to 2 jalapeño peppers
2 green onions
1/4 teaspoon minced garlic
4 ounces cream cheese
3/4 cup grated Parmesan cheese, divided
1/4 cup mayonnaise
1 teaspoon lemon juice

2 teaspoons soy sauce
4 1/4 grams kief or finely ground dry hash
1 (14-ounce) can water-packed artichoke
   hearts, drained
1/4 teaspoon cayenne pepper (optional)
Salt and pepper to taste
Crusty bread or crackers for serving

Preheat oven to 375 degrees F. In a food processor, combine jalapeños and green onions with the garlic and process until finely chopped. Add the cream cheese, 1/2 cup Parmesan, mayonnaise, lemon juice, soy sauce, and kief or hash and process until smooth. Add the drained artichoke hearts and process until coarsely chopped. Add the cayenne pepper, salt and black pepper and pulse to combine. Place in a small baking dish, or if preferred, a number of smaller baking dishes (ramekins work well). Sprinkle remaining cheese on top of dip. Bake about 25 minutes or until bubbly and top is beginning to brown. Serve hot with crusty bread or crackers for dipping.

Freezer Friendly!
Cover unbaked ramekins of dip tightly with foil and freeze. When ready to eat, bake in a preheated 375-degree F oven for about 45 minutes (timing will depend on portion size) or until bubbly and top is beginning to brown.

Hummus

This healthy Mediterranean dip is wonderful served with raw vegetables or triangles of pita bread. It also makes a great high-protein vegetarian sandwich spread.

Yield: 1 1/2 cups   Serving Size: 1/4 cup

1 (15-ounce) can garbanzo beans, rinsed and drained
1/4 cup plus 2 tablespoons tahini
1 1/2 grams kief or finely ground dry hash
1 teaspoon minced garlic
2 tablespoons minced fresh Italian parsley
3 tablespoon fresh lemon juice (juice of 1 large lemon)
3/4 teaspoon salt, or to taste
1/2 teaspoon black pepper, or to taste
1/4 teaspoon cayenne pepper, or to taste (optional)
1 tablespoon olive oil (optional)
1/4 teaspoon paprika (optional)

   In the bowl of a food processor combine garbanzo beans, tahini, kief or hash, garlic, Italian parsley, lemon juice, salt, pepper, and cayenne, if using. Process until smooth. If mixture is too thick, add a small amount of water, a tablespoon at a time, until you reach a consistency you like. Transfer to a serving bowl. If desired, make a small well in center of the dip and pour in olive oil and sprinkle with paprika. Use as a sandwich spread or as a dip for pita bread or raw vegetables.

 Tahini is a butter made from sesame seeds. Find it in health food stores, Middle Eastern markets, or most supermarkets. Don't be confused in the market—garbanzo beans and chickpeas are different names for the exact same legume.

Shrimp Rémoulade

Prepare the sauce for this shrimp appetizer up to 24 hours ahead of time so the flavors have time to develop.

Yield: 1 cup dressing   Serving Size: 6 shrimp plus almost 2 tablespoons dressing

1 gallon water
1/4 cup Cajun style shrimp/crab boil
48 jumbo tail-on shrimp
2 grams kief or finely ground dry hash
3/4 cup mayonnaise
3 tablespoons Creole mustard
   (substitute Dijon if you can't find Creole mustard)
1 1/2 teaspoons Worcestershire sauce
1/2 teaspoon Tabasco sauce
2 tablespoons finely diced green onions
2 tablespoons finely diced celery
2 tablespoons finely chopped fresh Italian parsley
1/2 teaspoon minced garlic
1 teaspoon lemon juice
Salt and black pepper to taste
Lettuce leaves for serving

In a large stockpot over medium-high heat, add water and shrimp boil and bring to a rolling boil. Add shrimp and stir for approximately 3 to 5 minutes. At this point, shrimp should be pink and curled. Pour off boiling water and replace with cold tap water to stop the cooking process. Drain and place shrimp in a serving bowl. Cover with plastic wrap and refrigerate until chilled.

Sprinkle kief over mayonnaise and stir well until combined. Stir in mustard, Worcestershire sauce, Tabasco sauce, green onions, celery, parsley, garlic and lemon juice until well blended. Season to taste with salt and pepper. Cover and refrigerate for at least 4 hours and up to 24 hours.

To serve, arrange boiled shrimp on a bed of lettuce leaves and top with sauce. Store extra sauce in the refrigerator for up to 3 days.

 Shrimp Boil is a mixture of seasoning ingredients added to boiling water to season shrimp or crabs. Find it in a well stocked supermarket with other Cajun items. Zatarain's is a commonly found brand.

Steamed Artichoke with Garlic Aioli

Garlic infused mayonnaise makes a perfect dip for either hot or chilled steamed artichoke. You can make the artichoke and aioli up to a day ahead of time and keep in the refrigerator until needed.

Yield: 1 artichoke plus 1/4 cup aïoli   Serving Size: 1/2 artichoke plus 2 tablespoons aïoli

1 large artichoke
1 tablespoon distilled white vinegar
1/4 cup mayonnaise
1 teaspoon lemon juice
1/2 gram kief or finely ground dry hash

1/4 teaspoon minced garlic
1/4 teaspoon black pepper
1/8 teaspoon cayenne (optional)
Salt to taste

Slice about 3/4-inch off the tip of the artichoke. Cut off excess stem, leaving about 1/2 inch, and remove any small leaves on the stem. Rinse artichoke in cold water.

Add the vinegar to a few inches of water in the bottom of a large pot. Put a steamer basket into the pot and place artichoke in it. Bring water to a boil over high heat, reduce heat to a simmer, and cook, adding water as necessary, until the outer leaves can be easily pulled off, about 25 to 30 minutes.

Prepare dip while artichoke cooks. Stir together mayonnaise and lemon juice in a small bowl. Sprinkle hash or kief over mayonnaise and stir until cannabis concentrate is evenly distributed. Stir in garlic, pepper, and cayenne, if using. Season to taste with salt.

Serve artichoke, either hot or chilled, with garlic aioli for dipping.

Deviled Eggs

An old-fashioned favorite, deviled eggs are just as popular today as they were in our grandparent's days.

Yield: 12 deviled egg halves   Serving Size: 2 deviled egg halves

6 hard-boiled eggs
3 tablespoons mayonnaise
3/4 teaspoon Dijon mustard
3/4 teaspoon prepared horseradish
3/4 teaspoon apple cider vinegar

1/4 teaspoon sugar
Salt and pepper to taste
1 1/2 grams kief or finely crumbled dry hash
1/8 teaspoon paprika

Cut eggs in half lengthwise and carefully scoop out the yolks into the bowl of a food processor. Add mayonnaise, mustard, horseradish, vinegar, sugar, salt, pepper, and kief or hash. Purée until mixture is smooth. Transfer contents of food processor to a pastry bag fitted with a star tip. Pipe egg yolk mixture into hollowed-out egg whites. Alternately, you can simply spoon the egg yolk mixture into the egg whites with a teaspoon. Sprinkle tops of eggs lightly with paprika. Refrigerate until ready to serve.

Bacon-Wrapped Stuffed Figs

These elegant appetizers pack a ton of flavor into a bite-sized package. Prepare up to a day ahead and keep refrigerated. Bake just before serving.

Yield: 8 stuffed figs   Serving Size: 2 stuffed figs

1 tablespoon mild goat cheese
1 tablespoon cream cheese
1/2 gram kief or finely ground dry hash

8 dried figs
8 toasted walnut or pecan halves
4 slices of bacon, halved crosswise

Preheat the oven to 400 degrees F. Beat together goat cheese and cream cheese until smooth. Sprinkle kief or hash over and mix until cannabis concentrate is evenly distributed in the cheese.

Cut a lengthwise slit in each fig and stuff with about 1/2 teaspoon of the cheese mixture and a toasted walnut or pecan half. Pinch the figs closed. Tightly wrap each fig in a piece of bacon and arrange seam side down on a wire rack set on a rimmed baking sheet. If you have trouble with bacon unwrapping, secure with a toothpick. Bake for 10 minutes. Use tongs to carefully turn each fig and then bake for about 10 minutes more or until bacon is browned and crisp. Serve warm.

Variation: Substitute dried dates for the figs.

Roast Beef Roll-Ups

Thinly sliced roast beef encases asparagus and a horseradish-spiked cream cheese filling for an easy-to-make finger food.

Yield: 12 roll-ups   Serving Size: 2 roll-ups

12 thick or 24 thin spears of asparagus
4 ounces cream cheese
1 tablespoon prepared horseradish
2 tablespoons minced green onions

1 1/2 grams kief or finely ground dry hash
Salt and pepper to taste
12 thin slices cold roast beef

Steam asparagus on the stovetop or in the microwave until barely cooked and still crisp in the center. Plunge into cold water to stop the cooking process and chill completely before continuing.

Whip cream cheese with an electric mixer until fluffy. Beat in horseradish and minced green onions. Sprinkle kief or ground dry hash over cream cheese and beat in until well combined. Season to taste with salt and pepper.

Spread a line of about 2 teaspoons cream cheese mixture down the center of a slice of roast beef. Place 1 thick or 2 thin steamed asparagus spears on the cream cheese and roll the roast beef around the asparagus and filling. Repeat with remaining ingredients. Serve immediately. Cover leftovers with plastic wrap and refrigerate for up to 1 day.

Mini Curry Samosas

Curry spices these tasty edible vegetarian packets. Using won ton wrappers makes preparation quick and easy. Freeze extras to cook up fresh anytime you want a flavorful medicated snack.

Yield: 32 samosas   Serving Size: 4 samosas

1 1/4 pounds baking potatoes
1 tablespoon olive oil
1 large onion, diced
1 1/2 teaspoons minced garlic
1 jalapeño or serrano chile pepper, minced
1 1/2 teaspoons minced fresh ginger
3/4 cup frozen peas
3/4 teaspoon ground dried coriander seeds

1 1/2 teaspoons curry powder
1/2 teaspoon sugar
1 teaspoon salt
3/4 teaspoon pepper
4 grams kief or finely ground dry hash
32 won ton wrappers
Vegetable oil for frying

Wash potatoes and cook in the microwave for 5 to 10 minutes (depending on size) or in a 350-degree F oven for 45 to 60 minutes or until tender. Let cool until you're able to handle. Split potatoes in half, scoop out the flesh into a large bowl, and discard skins. Set aside.

Heat olive oil in a large skillet over medium-high heat. Add onion and cook, stirring occasionally, for about 3 minutes or until translucent and just beginning to brown. Add garlic, chile pepper, ginger, and peas and cook, stirring, for 2 minutes. Add coriander, curry powder, sugar, salt and pepper. Stir to combine. Sprinkle in kief or hash and stir until well combined. Add contents of the skillet to the bowl with potatoes. Use a large spoon to stir and mix well until everything is combined.

Place a won ton wrapper on a clean surface and lightly moisten all 4 edges. Run a tablespoon of filling in a diagonal line down the middle. Pick up one corner and fold in to the center, so it looks like you are beginning to fold a paper airplane. Now start rolling, shaping the potato filling into a cone shape formed by rolling as you go. Hold the cone in your hand and push filling down. Moisten the top flap and fold down, sealing all edges. You should be left with what looks like a flat topped ice cream cone.

Heat oil in a deep fryer to 350 degrees F, or heat enough oil to cover in a deep pot or skillet. Fry samosas in a single layer (do not crowd) for about 2 minutes, turning once. Fry for another 2 minutes or until golden brown. Serve hot.

Freezer Friendly!
Freeze samosas flat on a waxed paper-lined baking sheet before removing to a plastic freezer storage bag. When ready to eat, fry frozen samosas as above. Use caution when adding frozen foods to hot oil—splatters can and do occur.

Crab Rangoon

Sweet crab and a spicy cream cheese mixture hide inside crisp fried won ton wrappers for a favorite party finger food that will disappear as fast as you can make it.

Yield: 32 crab rangoons   Serving Size: 4 crab rangoons

4 ounces cream cheese
2 grams kief or finely ground dry hash
2 teaspoons minced red onion
1 small green onion, minced
1/8 teaspoon minced garlic
1/2 teaspoon Worcestershire sauce
1 teaspoon soy sauce
4 ounces cooked or canned crab meat, drained and flaked
1 package won ton wrappers
Oil for deep-frying
Soy sauce and Asian-style hot sauce for serving

Place cream cheese in a large bowl and beat with an electric mixer at high until light and fluffy. Sprinkle kief or hash over cream cheese and beat in until cannabis concentrate is evenly distributed. Add minced red and green onions, garlic, Worcestershire sauce, and soy sauce and beat until all ingredients are combined. Stir in crab meat until evenly mixed.

Lay a won ton wrapper on a flat surface and place 1 teaspoon filling in the center. Lightly wet the edges of the wrapper. Fold wrapper over on a diagonal to form a small filled triangle. Crimp edges closed well—take extra care with this step to ensure filling doesn't leak out during frying. Repeat with remaining filling and wrappers; place prepared rangoons on a baking sheet. Cover completed appetizers with a damp paper towel as you work to prevent them from drying out.

Heat oil in a deep fryer or a wok to 350 degrees F. Fry rangoons, taking care not to overcrowd the fryer, until golden brown, turning once during cooking, about 2 to 3 minutes total. Drain on a wire rack and serve hot with soy sauce or Asian-style hot sauce for dipping.

Freezer Friendly!
Freeze uncooked rangoons on a waxed paper-lined baking sheet. When frozen, transfer to a plastic storage bag. When ready to eat, fry frozen rangoons in 350-degree F oil as above, about 3 to 4 minutes total. Use caution when adding frozen foods to hot oil as splatters can and do occur.

Shrimp and Pork Potstickers

Savory pork blends perfectly with sweet shrimp in these tasty little packets served pan-fried with a dipping sauce. I like to use Jimmy Dean light sausage, as the spices just seem to work and it's lower in fat than traditional sausage, but use your favorite kind. These dumplings are also terrific in soup. Simply add uncooked or frozen potstickers to simmering chicken stock.

Yield: 32 potstickers   Serving Size: 4 potstickers

1/2 pound pork sausage or light pork sausage
2 grams kief or finely ground dry hash, or
   3 grams finely ground bud
1/2 pound tiny cooked shrimp (or finely chop
   larger cooked shrimp)
1 large egg
1 large green onion, minced
2 teaspoons grated fresh ginger

1/4 teaspoon minced garlic
1 teaspoon sesame oil
1 1/2 teaspoons rice vinegar
1 1/2 teaspoons soy sauce or reduced-sodium
   soy sauce
1/2 teaspoon black or white pepper
32 won ton wrappers
Vegetable oil or canola oil for frying

    In a large mixing bowl combine sausage, kief, ground hash or ground bud, shrimp, egg, green onion, ginger, garlic, sesame oil, rice vinegar, soy sauce, and pepper. Use your hands to mix everything together until it is completely combined.

    Place about a teaspoon of filling in the center of a won ton wrapper. Use a pastry brush to wet the edges of the wrapper and fold diagonally to form a triangle. Pinch the edges well to seal. Bring the two side points to meet in the center, add a dab of water, and pinch them together. Repeat with remaining filling and wrappers. Place prepared dumplings on a waxed paper-lined baking sheet while working.

    Heat a small amount of vegetable or canola oil over medium-high heat in a skillet large enough to hold the amount you want to cook in a single layer with a little room to spare. Carefully add potstickers to skillet, taking care to avoid sputtering oil, and cook without moving for about 3 minutes or until bottoms are browned; carefully turn the dumplings. Add 1/2 cup water to the hot skillet and immediately cover. Reduce heat to medium and let dumplings steam for about 4 minutes or until cooked through. Serve with soy sauce for dipping.

Freezer Friendly!
Freeze leftover dumplings, uncooked, in a single layer on a waxed paper-lined baking sheet. Once frozen, remove to a lidded freezer container or plastic storage bag. Cook frozen potstickers as outlined above.

Asian Shrimp Salad Rolls

Translucent rice paper wrappers encase sweet shrimp and crunchy dressed salad in this light and healthy handheld appetizer. Since the salad inside is dressed, there's no need for a dipping sauce!

Yield: 6 rolls   Serving Size: 2 rolls

1/4 pound rice stick noodles
5 cups Asian salad mix greens
1 cup loosely packed chopped cilantro
1 small carrot, peeled and julienned
1 small cucumber, peeled, seeded, and julienned
2 tablespoons lime juice
1 tablespoon brown sugar
2 tablespoons Thai or Vietnamese fish sauce
2 tablespoons neutral canna-oil
1/2 teaspoon Sriracha hot sauce, more to taste
6 (8-inch) sheets Vietnamese rice paper
18 medium cooked peeled shrimp (about 1 pound)

Cook rice stick noodles according to package directions, set aside to cool.

In a large bowl, combine salad greens, cilantro, carrot, and cucumber and toss well to combine. In a separate small bowl, whisk together the lime juice, brown sugar, fish sauce, cannabis-infused oil, and Sriracha hot sauce. Toss dressing with vegetables to coat.

Soften a rice paper sheet by submerging it in very hot water for 3 to 5 seconds. Place on a damp paper towel. Place 3 shrimp in line down the center, leaving a 1/2-inch border at both ends. Place about 2 tablespoons cooked noodles down this line and top with 1/6 of the vegetable mixture. Fold up as you would a burrito—fold in the short ends of the wrapper and roll in a tight cylinder. Cover completed rolls with a damp paper towel as you prepare the remainder. Serve immediately.

 Vietnamese rice paper is made from drying rice paste on bamboo mats. **Fish sauce**, also known as *nam pla*, is a strong smelling and flavored sauce made from fermented fish. Find both ingredients in Asian markets or well stocked grocery stores.

Buffalo-Style Hot Wings

A buttery sauce, sharp with vinegar and hot peppers, give these savory wings their unforgettable flavor. If desired, serve with celery sticks and blue cheese dressing used for the Wedge Salad (page 52). Although it's not traditional, I also like to serve some crusty bread alongside it in order to get every drop of the medicated sauce.

Yield: 24 pieces   Serving Size: 4 pieces

3 pounds chicken wings
Oil for deep-frying
1 cup flour
1 teaspoon salt
1 1/2 teaspoons black pepper, divided
1 teaspoon plus 1/2 teaspoon garlic powder
1 teaspoon paprika
1/4 teaspoon cayenne pepper
1/4 cup unsalted butter
1/4 cup canna-butter
1/2 cup vinegar-based hot sauce such as Tabasco

Prepare chicken wings into "drummettes" by using poultry shears or a sharp knife to cut off wing tip at the first joint, then cut the wing again at the elbow joint. Discard tips or save for another purpose, such as making chicken stock.

Combine flour, 1 teaspoon each salt, pepper, garlic powder, paprika and 1/4 teaspoon (more to taste) cayenne pepper in a medium bowl. Stir to combine well. Use tongs to dip wings in flour mixture to lightly coat. Set aside on a wire rack and let rest for 5 minutes.

Heat oil in a deep fryer to 350 degrees F or heat enough oil to cover wings in a large deep skillet. Fry coated wings for about 10 minutes or until golden brown and meat is cooked through. If necessary, fry in batches so as not to overcrowd the skillet or fryer. Drain wings on a wire rack set over a baking sheet.

In a large skillet melt butter and cannabis-infused butter over medium-low heat. Stir in hot sauce, and 1/2 teaspoon each pepper and garlic powder. Stir together until mixture is well blended. Add fried chicken wings and toss to coat in sauce. Serve immediately with crusty bread to mop up any excess sauce.

Variation: Instead of frying, grill wings over a medium-hot fire for about 7 minutes per side or bake in a 400-degree F oven for about 20 minutes or until browned and cooked through. Proceed with sauce as above.

Mini Meatballs in Chile Sauce

Savory medicated meatballs swim in a smoky chipotle-infused chile-tomato sauce for a hot hors d'oeuvre or snack.

Yield: 48 meatballs plus sauce/8 servings   Serving Size: 6 meatballs

Sauce
3 dried pasilla or guajillo chiles
1 (28-ounce) can crushed tomatoes
2 or 3 canned chipotle peppers in
    adobo sauce, more to taste
1 tablespoon olive oil
1 medium white or yellow onion, finely diced
2 teaspoons minced garlic
3/4 teaspoon ground cumin
3/4 teaspoon ground coriander
3/4 teaspoon dried thyme
1 teaspoon dried oregano
Salt and pepper to taste
About 1/2 cup chicken stock or water

Meatballs
1 pound 80% lean ground beef
1/2 pound ground pork
1 medium white or yellow onion, finely diced
1 1/2 teaspoons minced garlic
1/4 teaspoon ground allspice
1 teaspoon ground cumin
1 teaspoon ground coriander
1 1/2 teaspoons oregano
3/4 teaspoon salt
1 teaspoon black pepper
1/2 cup dried bread crumbs
1 large egg
3 grams kief or finely ground dry hash, or
    4 grams finely ground bud
2 teaspoons olive or vegetable oil

Remove stems, seeds, and membranes from dried chiles and discard. Tear chiles into large flat pieces. Heat a large, preferably cast-iron skillet over high heat. Add chile pieces and toast for a minute per side to soften—do not brown. Purée chiles with the crushed tomatoes and their juices, chipotles, and a teaspoon or two of the adobo sauce in a food processor. Set aside.

Heat olive oil in a large Dutch oven over medium-high heat. Add onion and sauté for about 10 minutes or until just starting to brown. Add garlic, cumin, coriander, thyme, oregano, salt, and pepper and saute for another minute. Transfer contents of Dutch oven to the food processor. Purée until smooth. Add chicken stock or water, as necessary, to achieve a proper consistency—thick, but liquid enough to coat the meatballs. Cook sauce in the Dutch oven over medium-low heat, stirring occasionally while you prepare the meatballs.

Combine beef, pork, diced onion, garlic, allspice, cumin, coriander, oregano, salt, pepper, bread crumbs, egg, and hash, kief, or ground bud in a large bowl. Use clean hands to mix until all ingredients are well combined. Form into small balls, using about 1 1/2 tablespoons per meatball.

Return skillet to heat over medium-high heat and add 2 teaspoons oil. Add meatballs and cook just until starting to brown—do NOT cook them through. Cook in batches if necessary so as not to overcrowd the skillet. Add browned meatballs to the pot of simmering sauce. Cover and simmer on low, stirring occasionally, for about 20 minutes or until cooked through.

Freezer Friendly!
Cool completely. Package meatballs and sauce together in a plastic freezer bag. Reheat frozen or thawed meatballs and sauce on the stovetop over medium heat or in the microwave, stopping every minute to stir, until just heated through.

Gougères

Savory little cheese puffs make irresistible appetizers. Once you get familiar with the recipe, experiment using different cheeses or by adding flavors like a tablespoon or two of minced garlic, chives, or jalapeño peppers.

Yield: 20 puffs   Serving Size: 4 puffs

³/4 **cup shredded Gruyère or Swiss cheese**
¹/4 **cup grated Parmesan cheese**
¹/2 **cup water**
3 **tablespoons butter**
¹/4 **teaspoon salt**
¹/8 **teaspoon black pepper**
1 **gram kief or finely ground dry hash**
¹/2 **cup all-purpose flour**
2 **large eggs**

Preheat oven to 425 degrees F. Cover a baking sheet with parchment paper. Combine the Gruyère cheese and Swiss cheese.

Place water, butter, salt, pepper, and kief or hash in a medium saucepan and heat over medium heat until butter is melted and cannabis is dissolved and evenly dispersed. Dump in the flour all at once and stir vigorously with a wooden spoon until mixture pulls away from the side of the pan and forms a smooth ball. Remove from the heat. Let cool for 3 minutes. Beat in eggs, one at a time, stirring quickly to prevent eggs from cooking. The batter will appear lumpy at first, but will smooth out with beating. You can alternately do the step of beating in the eggs in a food processor, adding them one at a time. Fold ³/4 of the cheese into the mixture. Transfer mixture to pastry bag fitted with a plain wide tip (or no tip at all) and pipe small mounds about 1 tablespoon each onto the prepared baking sheet. Alternately use a spoon to make small mounds. Top each mound with a little additional cheese and bake for about 10 minutes. Reduce oven temperature to 375 degrees F and bake for about 12 more minutes or until browned and cooked through. Serve hot.

Freezer Friendly!
Place cooled baked gougères in a lidded freezer container or plastic freezer bag and freeze. To reheat, place frozen puffs on a parchment-lined baking sheet in a 375-degree F oven until crisp and heated, about 15 minutes.

Argentine-Style Empanadas

South America's version of the meat pie is filled with an unforgettable raisin-studded spiced beef filling.

Yield: 16 empanadas   Serving Size: 2 empanadas

Crust
1 1/2 cups all-purpose flour
1/2 cup unsalted butter
1/3 cup milk

Filling
2 tablespoons olive oil, divided
1/3 pound 80% to 85% lean ground beef
1/2 small yellow onion, finely chopped
1/2 small red, orange, or yellow bell pepper,
　　seeded and finely chopped
1 small jalapeño pepper, seeded and minced
1 teaspoon minced garlic

2 baby red potatoes, diced
1 tablespoon raisins, chopped
1/2 teaspoon capers, chopped
1/2 teaspoon cumin
1/2 teaspoon oregano
1/2 teaspoon paprika, preferably smoked
1 tablespoon minced fresh Italian parsley
2 grams kief or finely ground dry hash
Salt and pepper to taste

Glaze
1 egg
1 tablespoon milk

Prepare crust by placing flour and butter in a food processor. Pulse a few times until butter is cut into flour and mixture resembles coarse crumbs. Remove from food processor. Alternately, cut butter into flour with 2 knives. Add just enough milk so that mixture comes together to form a ball of dough. Pat into a disc, cover in plastic wrap, and refrigerate for at least 30 minutes.

Meanwhile, prepare the filling. Heat 1 tablespoon olive oil in a large skillet over medium heat. Add beef and brown, stirring and dividing it into crumbles, about 5 minutes. Remove beef from skillet and add remaining olive oil. Add the onion, bell pepper, and jalapeño and sauté until softened and beginning to brown, about 5 minutes. Add garlic and sauté for another minute. Add the diced potato, raisins, capers, cumin, oregano, paprika, and parsley. Return browned beef to skillet and stir to combine well. Sprinkle kief or hash over mixture and season to taste with salt and pepper. Stir and cook until cannabis concentrate is evenly combined. Remove from heat.

Preheat oven to 375 degrees F. Roll out dough to 1/8-inch thickness on a lightly floured surface. Use a 3 1/2-inch round cookie cutter (or a glass) to cut out 16 circles. Place about a tablespoon of filling on half of each circle. Fold the circle in half and use a fork to press along edges, tightly crimping the dough closed. Cut a 1-inch slit on the top of each empanada to allow steam to escape. Place on a baking sheet sprayed with cooking spray.

Beat together egg and 1 tablespoon milk. Brush empanadas lightly with glaze and bake until golden brown, about 25 minutes. Serve hot or at room temperature.

 Freezer Friendly!
Cool filling before assembling. Freeze unbaked, unglazed, in a single layer before moving to a freezer bag. Reheat frozen empanadas on a sprayed baking sheet for 10 minutes, brush with glaze and bake about 25 more minutes or until hot.

Sliders

Even Harold and Kumar would agree, these are the ultimate sliders. These little hamburgers are freezer friendly, so make up a double or triple batch for any time you need a satisfying medicated snack.

Yield: 14 sliders   Serving Size: 2 sliders

1 medium onion, chopped
1 pound lean ground beef
2 grams kief or ground dry hash
1 1/2 teaspoons garlic powder
1 teaspoon black pepper
14 dinner rolls or mini hamburger rolls
2 tablespoons ketchup
2 tablespoons yellow mustard
14 small slices American, Cheddar, or Jack cheese
14 round slices dill pickle

    If you intend to freeze any sliders, take the extra step to blanch the chopped onion before proceeding by cooking in boiling water for 1 minute. Drain and set aside. Blanching keeps frozen vegetables from leaching too much water upon thawing. If you don't intend to freeze any of the sliders, skip this step and use raw onions.

    In a medium bowl, mix together ground beef, kief or ground hash, garlic powder, and black pepper until all ingredients are evenly combined. Divide beef into 14 equal portions. Press each portion into a very thin round patty slightly larger than the circumference of the roll to allow for shrinkage. Stack patties between waxed paper.

    Open rolls and spread each half with a very thin smear of ketchup, the other half with a thin smear of mustard. Top half of each roll with a slice of cheese (if you plan on freezing sliders, see instructions below for cheese with frozen sliders). Top cheese with a sprinkling of chopped onions.

    Heat a large skillet or griddle over medium-low heat and spray with cooking spray. Cook burger patties for about 30 seconds per side or until just cooked through. Place cooked burger patty on roll, cover with other half of roll. Serve hot.

Freezer Friendly!
Add cheese later when ready to eat. Wrap cooked sliders in plastic wrap and store in a freezer bag. Remove wrap, place frozen sliders on a paper towel and microwave for 30 seconds. Add cheese and cook for another 30 seconds or until heated.

Soups

If you have access to kief or hash, medicating soups becomes a simple matter of stirring the concentrate into the hot soup to dissolve just before serving. Cream soups also make a great vehicle for carrying cannabis concentrates.

Cooking with cannabis-infused butter or oil makes the soup category a bit more challenging, although you will find some examples in this chapter. Not many soups use enough oil or butter to render a sufficient cannabis dose, and that's a good thing. Oily, greasy soup would be tough to choke down, after all. But the creative cook will find other ways. I suggest looking at things that go into the soup for inspiration. Find good examples of this in recipes like Albondigas.

Chilled Cucumber Avocado Soup

Here is a unique and refreshing chilled soup to start a meal on a hot summer day.

Yield: 4 cups   Serving Size: 1 cup

3/4 cup whole milk plain yogurt
1/2 cup sour cream
1 gram kief or finely ground dry hash
3 medium cucumbers, peeled and seeded
2 small avocados, peeled and pitted
3 green onions
1/4 cup chopped cilantro

3 tablespoons chopped fresh mint
2 tablespoons freshly squeezed lemon juice
1 tablespoon cider vinegar
1 1/2 teaspoons salt, more to taste
1/2 teaspoon black pepper, more to taste
1/8 teaspoon cayenne, more to taste (optional)

Combine yogurt, sour cream, and kief or hash in bowl of a blender or food processor. Process until smooth. Add cucumbers, avocados, green onions, cilantro, mint, lemon juice, vinegar, salt, pepper, and cayenne, if using, to the bowl. Process until smooth. If soup is too thick, thin out with a little water to achieve a consistency you like. Chill until ready to serve. Garnish with additional cilantro and/or mint leaves. Store leftovers for up to a day in the refrigerator.

Gazpacho

For the best flavor, make this healthy Spanish chilled vegetable soup in the height of summer when tomatoes are at their finest.

Yield: 6 cups   Serving Size: 1 cup

5 medium ripe tomatoes
1 medium cucumber, peeled and seeded
1 medium yellow, orange or red bell pepper
1 or 2 jalapeño peppers, cored, seeded,
   and minced (optional)
1 teaspoon minced garlic
2 tablespoons fresh minced Italian parsley
   or cilantro

1 (11 1/2- to 12-ounce) can tomato juice or
   V8 juice
1/4 cup red wine vinegar
1/4 cup canna-olive oil
Salt and black pepper to taste

Roughly chop (or use a food processor to roughly chop) tomatoes, cucumber, and bell pepper. Stir in minced garlic, parsley or cilantro, jalapeño, if using, tomato or vegetable juice, red wine vinegar, and cannabis-infused olive oil. Stir well to combine and integrate all ingredients. Season to taste with salt and pepper. Serve cold. Leftovers will keep for a day in the refrigerator.

Curried Carrot Soup

Exotic curry marries perfectly with sweet carrots for a sophisticated puréed soup.

Yield: 4 cups   Serving Size: 1 cup

3/4 cup half-and-half
1 gram kief or hash
1 tablespoon butter
1 tablespoon olive oil
1 large yellow or sweet onion, diced
7 medium carrots, peeled and roughly chopped
2 teaspoons curry powder
1/8 teaspoon cayenne, more to taste (optional)
1/2 teaspoon salt
4 cups chicken stock
Cilantro for garnish (optional)

In a small pan, heat half-and-half over low heat—do not boil. Stir in kief or hash and warm, stirring until cannabis concentrate is dissolved. Remove from heat and set aside.

In a large pot, heat butter and olive oil over medium-high heat. Add onion and sauté until softened, about 5 minutes. Add carrots, curry powder, cayenne, if using, and salt. Sauté, stirring occasionally, for 5 minutes more to soften carrots. Stir in stock and bring to a boil. Reduce heat to low and simmer until carrots are tender, about 20 minutes. Use an immersion blender (or a food processor or blender in batches), to purée soup until smooth. Return to pot over medium heat. Stir in half-and-half/cannabis mixture and cook, stirring, just until heated through.

Freezer Friendly!
Cool completely, package in plastic freezer bags or lidded freezer containers, and freeze. Reheat frozen or thawed soup in a pot on the stove over medium heat, stirring frequently, until just heated through.

Roasted Garlic and Onion Soup

It's hard to believe there is only a small amount of cream and no meat at all in this intensely flavored puréed soup. Roasting the garlic and onions mellows their sharpness while bringing out a concentrated meaty flavor.

Yield: 5 cups   Serving Size: 1 1/4 cups

Cloves from 1 head garlic, peeled
2 large yellow onions, peeled and
   cut into large chunks
2 tablespoons olive oil
1/3 cup heavy cream
1 gram kief or hash

3 3/4 cups chicken or vegetable stock
1/2 teaspoon dried sage
1/2 teaspoon dried thyme
2 teaspoons balsamic vinegar
Salt and pepper to taste
Fresh chives and croutons for garnish, optional

Preheat oven to 350 degrees F. Place peeled whole garlic cloves and onion chunks in a roasting pan large enough to hold them in a single layer. Add the olive oil and toss to coat. Roast, stirring once or twice, for about 1 hour or until browned and caramelized.

While vegetables are roasting, heat cream in a small pan over medium heat. Do not boil, and watch closely as this can take seconds. Remove from heat and stir in kief or hash until dissolved. Set aside.

Remove the roasting pan of vegetables from the oven and place over 2 burners on the stove set to medium heat. Add 2 cups of chicken stock and stir to scrape up any browned bits from the roasting pan. Cook for 5 minutes before transferring contents of the pan to a food processor or blender. Purée until smooth then transfer to a large pot over medium heat. (Exercise caution anytime you put hot liquids in a blender or food processor—never fill more than half-full and always use the lid in order to prevent the liquid from shooting out the top and causing burns.) Alternately use an immersion blender to purée the soup right in the pot. Add remaining chicken stock, sage, thyme, and balsamic vinegar and bring to a simmer. Remove from heat and stir in the cream/cannabis mixture. Divide among 4 bowls, garnish with chives and croutons, if desired, and serve hot.

 Freezer Friendly!
Cool completely and package in zip-top freezer bags or lidded freezer containers and freeze. Reheat frozen or thawed soup in a pot on the stove over medium heat, stirring frequently, until just heated through.

French Onion Soup au Gratin

For the best, most intensely flavored onion soup, take some time and brown the onions until they are a deep mahogany brown. Baked with a baguette slice and melted cheese, this is one hearty soup. Add a salad, and you have a terrific light meal.

Yield: 5 cups soup   Serving Size: 1 1/4 cups (plus bread and cheese)

2 tablespoons unsalted butter
1 tablespoon olive oil
1 large sweet onion, such as Maui or Vidalia
2 large shallots
2 large leeks, white and pale green parts only
1 tablespoon minced garlic
1/2 cup dry sherry
6 cups beef stock
1 teaspoon Worcestershire sauce
1 bay leaf
1 gram kief or hash
1 teaspoon balsamic vinegar
Salt and pepper to taste
4 slices French baguette (preferably day-old)
1 1/3 cup shredded Gruyère or Swiss cheese

Heat butter and olive oil in a large pot over medium heat. Add sweet onion, shallots, and leeks and sauté, stirring occasionally, until starting to brown, about 10 minutes. Reduce heat to low and continue to cook the onion, still stirring every 5 minutes or so to scrape brown bits from the bottom of the pan, until the onions are deep brown, about 20 minutes. Add garlic and sauté for another 2 minutes. Increase heat to medium-high and deglaze pan with the sherry, scraping up all the brown bits from the bottom. Cook until most of the sherry is gone, about 2 to 3 minutes, then add stock, Worcestershire sauce, and bay leaf. Bring to a boil, reduce heat to low, and simmer for about 30 minutes.

Preheat broiler. Remove bay leaf from soup. Stir in kief or hash until dissolved. Stir in balsamic vinegar. Remove soup from heat and divide among 4 ovenproof bowls. Arrange bowls on a baking sheet. Sprinkle half the cheese over the soup in the bowls. Add a baguette slice to each bowl and top with the remaining cheese. Place baking sheet of bowls under the broiler until cheese is melted and lightly browned, about 3 to 4 minutes. Serve immediately.

Freezer Friendly!
Cool soup completely then chill before assembling as above. Cover freezer-to-oven-safe bowl with foil and freeze. Bake frozen soup at 375 degrees until hot and cheese is melted and browned, about 45 minutes.

Cream of Butternut Squash Soup

Here's a sophisticated soup with a sweet, slightly spicy flavor that makes a perfect starter to a festive fall or winter holiday meal.

Yield: 6 cups   Serving Size: 1 1/2 cups

1/2 large butternut squash
1 1/2 teaspoons butter
1 1/2 teaspoons olive oil
2 large shallots, peeled and diced
1/2 teaspoon minced garlic
1/3 cup orange juice
2 1/2 cups chicken or vegetable stock
1 teaspoon curry powder
1/8 teaspoon cayenne, more to taste (optional)
Salt and pepper to taste
1 gram kief or ground hash
1/3 cup cream or half-and-half

Use a large chef's knife to cut squash in half. Use a spoon to scoop out seeds and a vegetable peeler to peel off the outer layer of the squash. Cut peeled squash into 1-inch chunks.

Heat butter and olive oil in a large stockpot over medium-high heat. Add shallots and garlic and sauté for 1 minute. Add cubed squash and cook, stirring frequently, for 3 minutes. Add orange juice, stir, and cook for another 2 minutes. Stir in stock, curry powder, and cayenne, if using. Stir to blend and season to taste with salt and pepper. Bring mixture to a boil, lower heat, cover, and simmer for about 45 minutes, stirring occasionally, or until squash is very tender. Sprinkle in kief or hash and cook, stirring, for another minute or 2 or until well mixed and dissolved. Remove from heat.

Use an immersion blender to purée the soup. Alternatively transfer soup, in batches, to a blender or food processor to purée. Add cream or half-and-half and purée or whisk to blend. Serve immediately.

Variations: Substitute cooked mashed pumpkin or other varieties of winter squash for the butternut squash.

Scottish Cock-A-Leekie Soup

Besides leeks, a milder member of the onion family, this traditional Scottish soup is intensely flavored with chicken.

Yield: 8 cups   Serving Size: 1 cup

1 1/2 pounds chicken parts
  (whatever is on sale)
1 medium onion, peeled and quartered
2 medium carrots, quartered
2 medium celery stalks, quartered
6 garlic cloves, peeled and crushed
2 bay leaves
1/2 teaspoon whole peppercorns
1 teaspoon dried thyme
6 cups chicken stock
1 tablespoon olive oil

2 large leeks, white and light green parts only,
  thinly sliced
1 large russet potato, peeled and diced
2 1/2 grams kief or hash
1/8 teaspoon cayenne, more to taste
1/8 teaspoon ground nutmeg
2 teaspoons fresh lemon juice
1/2 cup half-and-half
2 tablespoons minced chives
Salt and pepper to taste

In a large pot combine chicken pieces, onion, carrots, celery, garlic cloves, bay leaves, peppercorns, thyme, and chicken stock. If the chicken is not yet immersed, add enough cold water to cover it. Bring to a boil over medium-high heat. Reduce heat to low, partially cover, and simmer for about an hour. Use tongs to transfer chicken to a plate. When cool enough to handle, discard skin and bones and shred the meat. Set aside. Strain the stock and discard all solids. Skim off excess fat, if desired.

In same pot, heat olive oil over medium-high heat. Add leeks and sauté until softened and just starting to brown, about 5 minutes. Return stock to the pot along with the potato and bring to a boil. Reduce heat to medium-low and cook until potato is tender, about 20 minutes. Use an immersion blender to purée the soup (or transfer to a blender or food processor), leaving it partially chunky. Purée in batches if necessary. Return soup to pot. Stir in the kief or hash and cook on low, stirring, until cannabis is dissolved. Stir in cayenne, nutmeg, and lemon juice and return chicken to the pot. Stir in half-and-half and remove from heat. Ladle into bowls and garnish with fresh chives.

Freezer Friendly!
Cool completely and freeze extra soup and chicken in a lidded container or plastic freezer bag. Reheat frozen or thawed soup in a saucepan on the stovetop over medium-low heat until heated through.

Albondigas (Mexican Meatball Stew)

Mint adds a subtle yet unforgettable flavor to savory meatballs floating in a vegetable-laden broth in this traditional Mexican soup. For best results, get fresh mint if possible, but dried will do in a pinch.

Yield: 6 cups   Serving Size: 1 cup

Meatballs
1/3 cup fresh bread crumbs
3/4 pound lean ground beef
1 teaspoon minced garlic
1/2 teaspoon salt
1/2 teaspoon pepper
2 tablespoons finely chopped fresh mint, or
   1 teaspoon dried mint
1 large egg
1 1/2 grams kief or finely ground dry hash, or
   3 grams finely ground bud

Soup
1 teaspoon olive oil
1 medium onion, diced
1 large celery stalk, diced
2 medium carrots, peeled and sliced
1 jalapeño pepper, cored, seeded, and minced
1 teaspoon minced garlic
1 (14-ounce) can crushed tomatoes with
   green chiles
4 cups chicken stock
1 teaspoon dried oregano
1/3 cup loosely packed chopped cilantro leaves
1 1/2 teaspoons cider vinegar
Salt and pepper to taste

To make fresh bread crumbs, use a food processor to process a slice of your favorite bread. Any type of nonsweet bread will do: white, wheat, whole grain, baguettes, etc.

In a large bowl, combine bread crumbs with ground beef, 1 teaspoon minced garlic, 1/2 teaspoon each salt and pepper, minced mint, and egg. Sprinkle in kief or finely crushed dry hash or finely ground bud. Use clean hands to mix and combine all meatball ingredients well. Roll into small meatballs using about 1 tablespoon meat mixture per meatball. Set aside.

In a large soup pot heat 1 teaspoon olive oil over medium heat; add chopped onion, celery, carrots, and jalapeño and cook, stirring frequently, until softened, about 5 to 8 minutes. Add 1 teaspoon garlic and cook, stirring, for another minute before adding the tomatoes and their juice, chicken stock, and oregano. Stir the soup and bring to a boil. Add meatballs and reduce heat to a simmer. Cover the pot and simmer for 20 minutes. Stir in cilantro and vinegar. Simmer for another 10 minutes. Season to taste with salt and pepper. Serve garnished with fresh cilantro sprigs.

 Freezer Friendly!
Cool completely and package meatballs and soup together in a lidded freezer container. Reheat thawed or frozen soup in the microwave or thaw in fridge and heat on the stovetop over medium-low heat just until hot.

Salads & Salad Dressings

Salads are some of the easiest foods to medicate, or more specifically, salad dressings are. Most contain substantial amounts of oil that be swapped out for canna-oil. Toss any food with these, and you've instantly cannabinized it!

You'll find cannabis-infused versions of our most popular salad dressings at the end of this chapter. Keep in mind that you can also use the blue cheese dressing included with the Wedge Salad recipe and the Almost Caesar Salad dressing for other purposes, too.

Mayonnaise-based salads are best medicated by adding kief or hash to the mayonnaise before adding this ingredient to others in your recipe. If you feel so inclined, you can also make homemade mayonnaise using cannabis-infused oil. I haven't included a recipe here, as this would also include the use of raw eggs, something many patients shouldn't have due to concerns of possible salmonella and other food-born illnesses. If you have no immune system compromises and don't mind raw eggs, you can find many good mayonnaise recipes on the internet or in gourmet cookbooks, otherwise stick to commercial varieties and add cannabis concentrates.

Fruit Salad-Stuffed Cantaloupe

Colorful fruit salad fills a sweet cantaloupe bowl topped with creamy orange yogurt dressing.

Yield: 2/3 cup dressing   Serving Size: 1/3 cup dressing

1/2 cup plain whole milk yogurt
1/8 teaspoon ground cardamom
1/2 gram kief or finely ground dry hash
2 tablespoons frozen orange juice concentrate
1 tablespoon honey, more to taste

1/4 teaspoon vanilla extract
1 medium cantaloupe
2 cups mixed cut fresh fruit, such as berries,
    watermelon, bananas, grapes, etc.

Place yogurt in a medium bowl and sprinkle with cardamom and kief or finely ground hash. Mix until evenly distributed. Mix in frozen orange juice concentrate, honey, and vanilla and mix until smooth and all ingredients are incorporated into the yogurt. Refrigerate while you prepare the fruit.

Cut cantaloupe in half and remove seeds. Fill hollowed melon with mixed fresh fruit. Divide dressing over the fruit and serve immediately.

Wedge Salad with Blue Cheese Dressing

This classic retro salad boasts all the flavors of a BLT sandwich with the added benefits of creamy avocado, tangy blue cheese, and of course, cannabis.

Yield: 1 cup dressing   Serving Size: 1/4 cup dressing

Dressing
6 tablespoons sour cream
2 tablespoons buttermilk
1 tablespoon lemon juice
1 gram kief or finely ground dry hash
4 ounces crumbled blue cheese
1/4 teaspoon salt
1/2 teaspoon black pepper
2 tablespoons finely chopped chives

Salad
1 head iceberg lettuce
4 slices bacon, cooked and crumbled
2 large tomatoes, seeded and diced
2 medium avocados, peeled and diced

Prepare dressing by whisking together sour cream, buttermilk, and lemon juice in a small bowl. Sprinkle kief or hash over the mixture and whisk to combine. Stir in blue cheese, salt, pepper, and chives.

Wash lettuce and cut in quarters. Place one quarter on each of 4 salad plates. Drizzle dressing over lettuce wedges and sprinkle crumbled bacon, diced tomatoes and avocado on top and around the plate. Serve immediately.

Store leftover portions of dressing in the refrigerator for up to 3 days.

Almost Caesar Salad

I call this my "almost" Caesar salad because in deference to patients who may have immune system concerns, it contains no raw eggs. The flavor is so good you'll never miss this traditional ingredient. As written, the recipe is substantially dosed, provided you are using quality plant material to make your oil. Edible cannabis lightweights may want to adjust the olive oil to canna-oil ratio.

Yield: about 12 cups   Serving Size: 2 cups dressed salad

6 tablespoons canna-olive oil
2 tablespoons olive oil
1 tablespoon anchovy paste
2 tablespoons lemon juice
1/2 teaspoon minced garlic
1 teaspoon Dijon mustard
1 teaspoon Worcestershire sauce
2 large heads romaine lettuce, washed and chopped
3 ounces shaved or freshly grated Parmesan cheese
1 cup prepared croutons
Salt and pepper to taste

Place cannabis-infused olive oil, olive oil, anchovy paste, lemon juice, garlic, mustard, and Worcestershire sauce in a blender or food processor and purée. Alternately whisk ingredients by hand until combined and emulsified.

In a large bowl, toss together lettuce, Parmesan, and croutons with dressing. Season to taste with salt and pepper. Divide among 6 salad plates, preferably chilled, and serve immediately.

Pungent, salty **anchovy paste** is sold in tubes and can be found in Italian markets and the Italian section of most well stocked grocery stores.

Summer Grilled Corn Salad

Sweet summer corn gets a taste of smoke from the grill before blending with fresh veggies and a citrus dressing for a great summer side dish.

Yield: 6 cups   Serving Size: 1 cup

Salad
4 ears fresh corn, shucked
About 2 tablespoons olive oil
2 large ripe tomatoes, seeded and finely chopped
1/2 large red, yellow, or orange bell pepper, finely chopped
1 large jalapeño pepper, cored, seeded, and minced
2 large green onions, white and green parts, finely chopped
1/3 cup packed finely chopped cilantro

Dressing
1/4 cup lemon or lime juice
1/4 teaspoon minced garlic
1 teaspoon sugar
1/8 teaspoon cayenne, more to taste (optional)
3/4 teaspoon dried oregano
1/2 cup canna-olive oil
Salt and pepper to taste

Preheat a grill to medium heat. Brush shucked corn ears lightly with olive oil and place on the grill. Cook, turning frequently, until most corn kernels have started to brown, about 12 to 15 minutes. Allow corn to cool before proceeding.

Use a sharp knife to cut the grilled corn kernels from the cob into a large bowl. Add the tomatoes, bell pepper, jalapeño, green onions, and cilantro and toss to mix.

Place lemon or lime juice, garlic, sugar, cayenne, if using, oregano, and cannabis-infused olive oil in a blender or food processor and process until mixed and emulsified. Alternately, whisk ingredients in a medium bowl until emulsified. Pour dressing over salad and toss to mix and coat. Season to taste with salt and pepper. Serve immediately or chill. Store leftovers up to 2 days in the refrigerator.

Cucumber and Sweet Onion Salad

This refreshing creamy cucumber salad goes together in minutes and makes a great accompaniment for grilled meats. Using mint or dill will change the flavor substantially, but both work well.

Yield: 2 cups   Serving Size: 1/2 cup

1/4 cup sour cream
3/4 teaspoon lemon juice
1 gram kief or finely ground dry hash

2 thin slices sweet onion
1 large cucumber, peeled and thinly sliced
2 tablespoons minced fresh mint or dill

In a small bowl, whisk together sour cream, lemon juice, and kief or finely ground hash until smooth and well mixed. Quarter the onion slices and toss in the bowl along with the cucumber slices and minced mint or dill. Toss to coat vegetables and evenly mix all ingredients. Serve immediately.

Creamy Coleslaw

Make this traditional coleslaw with both red and green cabbage for a colorful dish that brightens up any table.

Yield: 4 cups   Serving Size: 1 cup

1/4 teaspoon minced garlic
1/4 teaspoon sugar
1 tablespoon lemon juice
3 tablespoons mayonnaise
1 gram kief or finely ground dry hash

3 cups shredded cabbage, green,
    red, or a mix of both
1 medium carrot, grated
2 tablespoons grated onion
Salt and pepper to taste

In a medium bowl, mix together garlic, sugar, lemon juice, and mayonnaise until well blended. Sprinkle kief or ground dry hash over mayonnaise mixture and stir to combine the cannabis into the dressing.

In a large bowl, toss together shredded cabbage, carrot, and onion. Add dressing, then toss to evenly coat the vegetables. Season to taste with salt and pepper. Refrigerate until ready to serve. Best made several hours ahead of time. Leftovers will keep in the refrigerator for up to 3 days.

Asian-Style Slaw

Slaw gets an Asian-inspired makeover using mild Napa cabbage, toasted almonds, and a sesame and soy-flavored dressing.

Yield: 4 cups   Serving Size: 1 cup

Dressing
1/3 cup mayonnaise
1 1/2 teaspoons sugar
1 gram kief or finely ground dry hash
1 tablespoon rice vinegar
1 1/2 teaspoons lemon juice
1 1/2 teaspoons soy sauce
1 teaspoon sesame oil
1/4 teaspoon Sriracha hot sauce, more to taste (optional)
2 teaspoons grated fresh ginger

Salad
1/2 cup sliced almonds
4 cups shredded Napa cabbage, 1/2 small head
3/4 cup thinly sliced radishes, about 1 small bunch
3/4 cup thinly sliced green onions, about 3 large
3/4 cup finely chopped cilantro leaves
Salt and pepper to taste

　　Place mayonnaise in a small bowl and sprinkle sugar and kief or hash over the surface. Stir until sugar and cannabis concentrate is evenly distributed in the mayonnaise. Whisk in vinegar, lemon juice, soy sauce, sesame oil, hot sauce, if using, and grated ginger. Set dressing aside while you prepare the salad.

　　Place almonds in a dry, preferably cast-iron skillet over medium heat. Toast, stirring occasionally, until golden brown, about 6 to 8 minutes. Set aside to cool while you chop remaining vegetables.

　　In a large bowl, toss together the Napa cabbage, radishes, green onions, cilantro and toasted almonds until well mixed. Pour dressing over salad and toss until ingredients are well coated. Season to taste with salt and pepper.

Best-Ever Potato Salad

I've been making a nonmedicated version of this potato salad for decades, just as my father did before me. No matter how much I make, it always disappears at every gathering, even if the crowd is small.

Yield: 6 cups   Serving Size: 1 cup

2 1/2 pounds russet potatoes
2 tablespoons cider vinegar
2 teaspoons Dijon mustard
1/2 cup mayonnaise
1/2 teaspoon sugar
1/2 teaspoon salt
1/2 teaspoon black pepper
1 1/2 grams finely ground dry kief or hash
1 large celery stalk, finely diced
1/2 medium yellow onion, finely diced
3 hard-boiled eggs, peeled and chopped
1/4 cup finely chopped cilantro or Italian parsley

    Peel potatoes and cut into 2-inch chunks. Bring a large pot of salted water to a boil over high heat. Add potatoes and cook just until tender, about 7 minutes. Do not cook to mush. Drain and set aside.

    In a small bowl combine vinegar, mustard, mayonnaise, sugar, salt, and pepper. Whisk to combine. Sprinkle in kief or finely ground dry hash and whisk to combine. Set aside.

    Place drained potatoes in a large bowl along with the celery, onion, hard-boiled eggs, and cilantro or parsley. Add the dressing and toss gently to combine the ingredients and coat the potatoes in the dressing. Chill until ready to serve. Salad can be made up to a day ahead of time.

Grilled Vegetable Quinoa Salad

Fire-grilled vegetables mix with nutty super grain quinoa and a flavor-filled balsamic dressing for a side dish salad that packs well for picnics or lunches.

Yield: 4 cups   Serving Size: 1 cup

1 1/2 teaspoons minced garlic, divided
1/4 cup olive oil
1 medium zucchini
1 large red, yellow, or orange bell pepper
1 large onion
8 ounces mushrooms
1 cup water
1/2 cup quinoa
2 tablespoons balsamic vinegar
1/4 teaspoon Dijon mustard
1 teaspoon Italian seasoning
3 tablespoons canna-olive oil
Salt and pepper to taste

Mix garlic and olive oil in a small bowl. Cut ends off zucchini and cut into 1-inch rounds. Core and seed bell pepper and cut into 2-inch chunks. Wash mushrooms. Thread vegetables onto wooden skewers. Brush with garlic oil. Grill vegetables over a medium hot fire, turning to grill on all sides, about 20 to 25 minutes. Remove vegetables from heat, take off skewers, cool slightly, and chop into 1/2-inch chunks.

Bring a cup of water to a boil in a small saucepan over medium heat. Stir in quinoa, reduce heat to low, cover and simmer until cooked, about 10 minutes.

Prepare dressing by whisking together vinegar, mustard, Italian seasoning, and cannabis-infused oil until combined and emulsified.

In a large bowl, toss together cooked quinoa and chopped grilled vegetables. Pour in dressing and toss to coat. Serve hot, at room temperature, or cold. Store leftover salad in the refrigerator for up to 3 days.

 Quinoa (pronounced *keen-wah*) is a tiny, bead-shaped, nutritious grain that expands to about four times its volume during cooking. Quinoa is lower in carbohydrates and higher in unsaturated fats than most grains and higher in protein than all others.

Tabouli

Hearty whole grain bulghur wheat mixes with herbs and veggies in this classic Middle Eastern salad.

Yield: 4¹/₂ cups   Serving Size: 3/4 cup

1 1/3 cups boiling water
1 1/2 teaspoons salt
3/4 cup dry bulghur wheat
3/4 cup minced green onions
1 1/2 cups diced seeded ripe tomatoes
1/4 cup finely chopped fresh mint
3/4 cup finely chopped Italian parsley
2 teaspoons minced garlic
1/3 cup canna-olive oil
5 tablespoons freshly squeezed lemon juice
Salt and pepper to taste

    Combine boiling water, 1 1/2 teaspoons salt, and bulghur in a large bowl. Cover and let stand for 15 minutes or until water is absorbed and bulghur has softened.

    Stir in green onions, tomatoes, mint, Italian parsley, garlic, cannabis-infused olive oil, and lemon juice and mix until ingredients are evenly combined. Season to taste with additional salt and pepper if needed. Chill until ready to serve. Best made several hours ahead of time. Leftovers will keep for up to 4 days in the refrigerator.

Italian-Style Tuna and White Bean Salad

Canned tuna fish pairs with delicate white beans in this fiber-rich, mayonnaise-free Italian tuna salad.

Yield: 2 cups plus salad greens   Serving Size: 1 cup plus greens

1 (5- or 6-ounce) can tuna, preferably
   packed in olive oil, drained
1 (15-ounce) can white beans,
   rinsed and drained
1/4 cup minced yellow onion
1/4 cup minced celery

3 tablespoons minced fresh Italian parsley
1 tablespoon lemon juice
2 tablespoons canna-olive oil
1/2 teaspoon minced garlic
Salt and pepper to taste
2 cups salad greens for serving (optional)

In a large bowl, toss together the drained tuna, beans, onion, celery, and parsley until well mixed. In a small bowl, whisk together the lemon juice, cannabis-infused olive oil, garlic, salt, and pepper. Toss dressing with tuna mixture until all ingredients are well combined. Place 1 cup salad greens on each of 2 plates and top with tuna bean salad. Serve immediately. Store leftovers in the refrigerator for up to 2 days.

Classic Italian Vinaigrette

This dressing goes well on most any kind of tossed salad or cold vegetable salad including pasta, grain, or bean salads. For a change, try it on hot foods, too, like simple steamed fish or vegetables.

Yield: 3/4 cup/6 servings   Serving Size: 2 tablespoons

1/4 teaspoon minced garlic
1/4 cup red or white wine vinegar
1 tablespoons minced shallot
1/2 teaspoon Dijon mustard
3/4 teaspoon dried basil

3/4 teaspoon dried oregano
1/2 teaspoon black pepper, more to taste
Salt to taste
6 tablespoons canna-olive oil
2 tablespoons olive oil

Combine all ingredients except cannabis-infused oil and olive oil and whisk to blend. Pour in oils in a slow, steady stream while whisking vigorously in order to mix and emulsify the dressing. Alternately combine all ingredients in a food processor and purée or place in a shaker bottle and shake until combined. Refrigerate extra portions for up to 4 days.
    Variation: For **Parmesan Vinaigrette**, add 1/4 cup finely grated Parmesan cheese to the mix above.

Buttermilk Ranch Dressing

Of course ranch dressing is terrific on salads. But it's also a great dip for all kinds of fried foods or to dress chicken wings.

Yield: 1/2 cup/4 servings   Serving Size: 2 tablespoons

1 gram kief or finely ground hash
3 tablespoons mayonnaise
1/3 cup whole milk buttermilk
1/4 teaspoon minced garlic

2 tablespoons lemon juice
2 teaspoons minced cilantro or parsley
2 teaspoons minced chives
Salt and pepper to taste

In a medium bowl, sprinkle kief or ground hash over mayonnaise. Mix well until cannabis is evenly distributed in mayonnaise. Whisk in buttermilk and then stir in remaining ingredients. Store leftovers in the refrigerator for up to 3 days.

Asian-Style Vinaigrette

Use this Asian-style vinaigrette on mixed greens, over Chinese chicken salad, on steamed vegetables, or anytime you want to give a dish a little Asian inspiration.

Yield: 3/4 cup/6 servings   Serving Size: 2 tablespoons

1/4 teaspoon minced garlic
1/4 cup rice vinegar
1 tablespoons grated fresh ginger
1/2 green onion (white part), finely minced
1 tablespoon soy sauce

1 tablespoon toasted sesame seeds
1/2 teaspoon black pepper, more to taste
Salt to taste
1 teaspoon sesame oil
6 tablespoons neutral canna-oil

Combine all ingredients except sesame oil and cannabis-infused oil in a bowl and whisk to blend. Pour in oils in a slow, steady stream while whisking vigorously in order to mix and emulsify the dressing. Alternately combine all ingredients in a food processor and purée or place in a shaker bottle and shake until combined. Refrigerate extra portions for up to 4 days.

Variation: For **Thai-Style Salad Dressing**, leave out the ginger and substitute lime juice for the rice vinegar and fish sauce for the soy sauce. Add 1 teaspoon (more to taste) Sriracha hot sauce (optional).

Honey Mustard Dressing

Not only is honey mustard dressing terrific on salads, it also makes a great sandwich spread—especially for ham sandwiches.

Yield: ³/₄ cup/6 servings   Serving Size: 2 tablespoons

2 tablespoons lemon juice
1 tablespoon apple cider vinegar
2 teaspoons honey
2 teaspoons whole grain mustard
Salt and black pepper to taste
6 tablespoons canna-olive oil

   Combine all ingredients except cannabis-infused oil and whisk to blend. Pour in oil in a slow, steady stream while whisking vigorously in order to mix and emulsify the dressing. Alternately combine all ingredients in a food processor and purée or place in a shaker bottle and shake until combined. Refrigerate extra portions for up to 6 days.

Thousand Island Salad Dressing

Besides dressing salad, use Thousand Island dressing as a spread for sandwiches and burgers, or as a dip for chilled boiled shrimp.

Yield: ³/₄ cup/6 servings   Serving Size: 2 tablespoons

1 ¹/₂ grams kief or finely ground dry hash
¹/₂ cup mayonnaise
¹/₄ cup ketchup or chili sauce
1 hard-boiled egg, finely chopped
2 tablespoons pickle relish
1 tablespoon minced shallot
1 tablespoon minced chives or green onions
1 tablespoon minced fresh Italian parsley
Salt and pepper to taste

   In a medium bowl, sprinkle kief or ground hash over mayonnaise and stir until cannabis is evenly combined into the mayonnaise. Stir in remaining ingredients until evenly combined. Store leftovers tightly covered in the refrigerator for up to 3 days.

Brunch & Lunch

Morning snacks, light meals, and casual fare are what you'll find in this chapter. While these recipes are popular lunches, that doesn't mean you can't use then at other times of day, too.

When looking for brunch items from your own recipe collection to medicate, look to baked goods like muffins and coffee cake recipes that can be medicated by swapping in marijuana-infused butter or oil. At lunchtime, sandwich spreads and salad dressings make for easy ways to add cannabis to your foods.

Cranberry Applesauce Bread

Serve this simple moist cake, studded with tart ruby red cranberries, with morning or afternoon coffee or tea or as a late-night snack. Sprinkling brown sugar and cinnamon on top gives these little treats a wonderful crunchy crust.

Yield: 7 mini loaves   Serving Size: 1 mini loaf

6 tablespoons canna-butter
2 tablespoons unsalted butter
2 cups all-purpose flour
2 teaspoons baking powder
1/2 teaspoon salt
2 teaspoons cinnamon, divided
1/2 teaspoon nutmeg
1 large egg
1 cup unsweetened applesauce
1/2 cup, plus 3 tablespoons packed brown sugar
3/4 teaspoon vanilla extract
1 cup sweetened dried cranberries
1/2 cup chopped walnuts or pecans, optional

Preheat oven to 350 degrees F. Grease 7 mini loaf pans (2 3/4 × 3 3/4) with vegetable shortening or spray generously with cooking spray (if you use other size pans, just keep in mind that this recipe makes 7 total servings). Melt canna-butter and butter together over low heat in a small pan.

In a medium bowl, stir together flour, baking powder, salt, 1 1/2 teaspoons cinnamon, and nutmeg. In a large bowl, whisk together egg, applesauce, 1/2 cup brown sugar, melted butters, and vanilla extract. Stir in dry ingredients until just combined; batter will be somewhat lumpy. Stir in dried cranberries and nuts, if using. Divide batter among prepared loaf pans, filling each about 2/3 full. Combine remaining 3 tablespoons brown sugar and 1/2 teaspoon cinnamon and lightly sprinkle over the tops of loaves. Bake for about 20 to 25 minutes or until a toothpick inserted in the center of a loaf comes out clean. Cool in pan for 10 minutes before removing to a wire rack. Serve warm or at room temperature.

 Freezer Friendly!
Wrap extra applesauce bread tightly in plastic wrap or foil and freeze. Bring to room temperature and enjoy when ready to eat.

Chocolate Chip Banana Bread

Sweet bananas and chocolate go together perfectly for a casual anytime cake that needs no frosting. If you consider yourself a cannabis lightweight, make this recipe using just the cannabis-infused butter for a light dose. Otherwise, use the canna-butter along with kief or hash for a stronger dose.

Yield: 7 mini loaves   Serving Size: 1 mini loaf

1/4 cup canna-butter, softened
1 gram kief or hash (optional,
   see note above)
3/4 cup all-purpose flour
1/2 cup whole wheat flour
1/4 cup sugar
1/4 cup packed brown sugar
1/2 teaspoon salt
1/2 teaspoon baking powder

1/2 teaspoon baking soda
1/2 teaspoon nutmeg
1 1/2 cups mashed bananas
   (about 4 medium bananas)
1/4 cup buttermilk
2 tablespoons honey
1 large egg
1 teaspoon vanilla extract
3/4 cup chocolate chips

Preheat oven to 350 degrees F. Grease 7 mini-loaf pans (2 3/4 × 3 3/4) with vegetable shortening or spray generously with cooking spray (if you use other size pans, just keep in mind that this recipe makes 7 total servings).

If you plan on using kief or hash to augment this recipe, sprinkle over the softened canna-butter and beat to mix well. Set aside.

In a medium bowl, combine all-purpose flour, whole wheat flour, sugar, brown sugar, salt, baking powder, baking soda, and nutmeg and stir to mix. In a large bowl, combine bananas, buttermilk, canna-butter, honey, egg, and vanilla and beat well with an electric mixer or by hand. Add the dry ingredients and beat until just combined; do not overmix. Stir in chocolate chips. Fill pans slightly more than half-full (using about 1/2 cup batter per mini loaf). Bake until a toothpick inserted into the center of the loaf comes out clean, about 20 to 25 minutes. Cool in pans on a wire rack for 10 minutes before removing to a wire rack. Serve warm or at room temperature.

 Freezer Friendly!
Wrap extra banana bread tightly in plastic wrap or foil and freeze. Bring to room temperature and enjoy when ready to eat.

Carrot Bran Muffins

Sweet carrots combine with nutty bran flakes cereal to make these hearty muffins.

Yield: 12 muffins   Serving Size: 1 muffin

1 cup whole or low-fat milk
1/2 cup neutral canna-oil
1 large egg
1 cup shredded carrots
2 teaspoons finely grated orange zest
1 1/2 cups crushed bran flakes cereal
1 1/2 cups all-purpose flour
1 tablespoon baking powder
1/3 cup sugar
1/3 cup firmly packed brown sugar
1/2 teaspoon salt
3/4 teaspoon ground cinnamon
1/2 teaspoon dried ginger
1/4 teaspoon ground nutmeg
1/4 teaspoon ground cloves
1/4 teaspoon ground cardamom

Optional Add-Ins
1 cup raisins, sweetened dried cranberries,
    dried cherries, or dried blueberries
3/4 cup chopped walnuts or pecans

Preheat the oven to 375 degrees F. Grease 12 regular sized muffin cups or line with paper baking liners.

In a small bowl, whisk together milk, cannabis-infused oil, egg, carrots, and orange zest until combined. In a large bowl, combine crushed bran flakes, flour, baking powder, sugar, brown sugar, salt, cinnamon, ginger, nutmeg, cloves, and cardamom. Add wet ingredients to dry and stir just until all flour is moistened. Batter will be lumpy. Stir in any optional add-ins you are using and spoon batter into the prepared muffin cups, filling each about 3/4 full. Bake until tops have browned and toothpick inserted into the center comes out clean, about 25 minutes. Serve warm, or cool on a wire rack for later use.

Freezer Friendly!
Well wrapped muffins freeze well. Stack between layers of waxed paper and store in plastic freezer bags. Thaw at room temperature and serve.

Lemon Raspberry Scones

Sweet raspberries are countered by tart lemons in both the pastry and the glaze for a fabulous treat to serve with afternoon tea or anytime. For a variation, substitute the raspberries with blueberries or blackberries.

Yield: 10 scones   Serving Size: 1 scone

Scones
2 cups all-purpose flour
2 1/2 teaspoons baking powder
1/2 teaspoon salt
1/4 cup sugar
1/2 teaspoon ground cardamom
1 tablespoon lemon zest (zest of 1 lemon)
5 tablespoons cold canna-butter,
    cut into chunks

1 cup heavy cream, plus more for brushing
    before baking
1 cup frozen raspberries

Glaze
1/3 cup lemon juice
2 1/2 cups confectioners' sugar
2 tablespoons heavy cream

Preheat oven to 400 degrees F. Cover a baking sheet with a piece of parchment paper.

Place flour, baking powder, salt, sugar, cardamom, and lemon zest in the bowl of a food processor and pulse one or two times to mix. Add cold cannabis-infused butter and pulse a few times until mixture forms coarse crumbs. Add the cream and pulse a few times just until incorporated. Remove dough from food processor and place in a large bowl. Fold in berries. Gather dough into a disc, wrap in plastic wrap, and refrigerate for at least 30 minutes. Alternately use a pastry blender to cut the butter into the dry ingredients and mix in cream by hand before folding in berries.

Roll dough to about 1/2-inch thickness on a lightly floured surface. Use a 3 1/2-inch round cutter to cut out circles. Place on prepared baking sheet. Brush tops of scones with a little cream and bake for about 15 minutes or until tops are lightly browned. Let cool completely before applying glaze.

Prepare glaze by mixing lemon juice, confectioners' sugar and heavy cream until smooth. Pour glaze over cooled scones.

 Freezer Friendly!
Wrap extra baked glazed scones individually in plastic wrap, place in a plastic freezer bag, and freeze. Bring to room temperature and enjoy.

Cinnamon Rolls with Cream Cheese Icing

There's nothing as wonderful as the aroma of baking cinnamon rolls filling the house, except possibly the taste of freshly made hot cinnamon rolls.

Yield: 10 cinnamon rolls   Serving Size: 1 cinnamon roll

Rolls
3 cups flour
2 tablespoons nonfat dry milk powder
1 1/2 cups buttermilk
1/2 cup melted canna-butter
1 tablespoon yeast
1/4 cup sugar
1 large egg
1/2 cup brown sugar

2 tablespoons cinnamon
1/2 cup raisins (optional)
1/2 cup melted unsalted butter

Icing
4 ounces cream cheese
1/4 cup unsalted butter
1 3/4 cups confectioners' sugar
1 teaspoon vanilla extract

Stir together flour and nonfat milk powder, set aside.

Heat buttermilk and canna-butter in a small saucepan over low heat until butter is melted. Place in the bowl of a large food processor and cool to lukewarm. Sprinkle in yeast and sugar and pulse once or twice to mix. Let sit for 5 minutes. Add egg to food processor and pulse to mix. Add flour mixture and process until a ball of dough forms. Run machine for another minute or so to knead. Alternately mix dough in a stand mixer fitted with the dough hook. Place dough in a buttered bowl. Turn to coat, cover with a clean kitchen towel, and let rise in a draft-free spot until doubled, about 1 hour.

While cinnamon rolls are rising, prepare icing by beating together cream cheese and 1/4 cup butter until light and fluffy. Gradually beat in confectioners' sugar followed by vanilla. Continue to beat until frosting is smooth.

Preheat oven to 350 degrees F. Butter a 9×13-inch baking pan. In a small bowl, combine brown sugar, cinnamon, and raisins, if using.

Punch dough down. Let rest for 5 minutes, then roll on a lightly floured surface into a rectangle approximately 13×15.   Brush surface of dough with melted butter. Sprinkle brown sugar mixture over surface of dough. Starting at a long end, roll jellyroll style. Trim ends even and slice into 10 rolls about 1 1/2-inches wide. Arrange cut side up in prepared pan. Cover with a kitchen towel and let rise for 40 minutes. Bake for about 35 minutes or until golden brown. Let rolls cool for at least 10 minutes before spreading with icing and serving.

Freezer Friendly!
Freeze unbaked rolls in pan. Let pan sit at room temperature until dough is thawed and at room temperature and slightly risen. Bake as above. Left on the counter when you go to bed, they're usually ready to bake in the morning.

Mini Ham and Cheese Quiches

Mini muffin pans make it easy to make tiny, bite-sized quiches that you can pair with a salad for a light entrée or serve as appetizers. Instead of appetizers, turn this recipe into a brunch or lunch entrée by making one big 9-inch pie instead of using a mini muffin pan. You can also substitute diced cooked bacon for the ham.

Yield: 24 mini quiches   Serving Size: 4 quiches

3/4 cup half-and-half
3 grams kief or finely ground dry hash
2 tablespoons butter
2 tablespoons vegetable shortening
3/4 cup all-purpose flour
4 tablespoons milk

1/4 pound diced smoked ham
3 ounces Swiss cheese, shredded
2 large eggs
1/4 teaspoon salt
1/4 teaspoon pepper
1/8 teaspoon grated nutmeg

Preheat oven to 375 degrees F. In a small saucepan, heat half-and-half over low heat—do not boil. Sprinkle in kief or finely ground hash and stir until dissolved. Set aside to cool.

Prepare crust by cutting butter and shortening into flour by pulsing 8 to 10 times in a food processor until well combined. You can alternatively use a pastry blender to accomplish this, but prepare to spend more time at it. Transfer mixture from processor to a large bowl and stir in 4 tablespoons milk until dough just holds together. Gather into a ball, flatten into a disc, and refrigerate for at least 30 minutes.

Roll out crust to 1/8-inch thickness on a lightly floured surface. Use a 2 1/2-inch round cookie cutter or a small glass with an opening about that size to cut 24 circles from dough, rerolling as necessary. Press each circle into a mini muffin cup—dough should cover bottom and side with no overhang. Repeat with remaining dough and muffin cups.

Sprinkle finely diced ham into bottom of each dough-lined cup, about 1/2 teaspoon per cup. Sprinkle about 3/4 teaspoon shredded cheese into each cup on top of ham.

Whisk together eggs, cooled half-and-half/cannabis mixture, salt, pepper, and nutmeg until well combined. Pour egg mixture into muffin cups until just filled. Bake for about 40 minutes or until quiches are set and tops are golden brown. Cool for 5 minutes before removing from pans. Serve hot, warm, at room temperature, or even cold.

Freezer Friendly!
Stack cooled mini quiches between waxed paper in a large lidded rigid side freezer container and freeze. Microwave 4 frozen mini quiches for about 40 seconds or heat in a 375-degree F oven for about 40 to 45 minutes.

Eggs Benedict

Everyone's favorite indulgent brunch item—poached eggs and smoky Canadian bacon atop a toasted English muffin drizzled in rich lemony hollandaise sauce—sounds like it would be difficult and time consuming to make. Not so, as this easy-to-make recipe proves. You can use the versatile medicated hollandaise sauce for lots of other foods, too. Try it on simple steamed, poached, or grilled fish dishes or steamed veggies. Store leftover hollandaise sauce in a tightly covered container in the refrigerator for up 3 days. Reheat in the top of a double boiler or in a metal bowl suspended over barely simmering water, stirring constantly, until just heated. This is a delicate sauce that will break down in the microwave or over direct heat.

Yield: 2 servings   Serving Size: 2 Benedict muffin halves and 1/2 the sauce

Hollandaise Sauce
1/2 cup butter
1/2 gram kief or hash
3 egg yolks
2 tablespoons freshly squeezed lemon juice
1/4 teaspoon salt
1/4 teaspoon pepper
1/8 teaspoon cayenne pepper

Benedict
1 teaspoon white vinegar
4 large eggs
2 English muffins, split into halves
4 slices Canadian bacon
Paprika or dried parsley for garnish (optional)

Prepare hollandaise sauce by heating butter and kief or hash together in a small saucepan over medium-low heat, stirring until cannabis is dissolved in the butter. Heat, stirring, until butter is bubbly, but do not brown. Place egg yolks, lemon juice, salt, pepper, and cayenne in the bowl of a food processor or jar of a blender and process at high speed for 2 to 3 seconds. While processor or blender is running, drizzle in melted butter in a slow, steady, thin stream.

Fill a large saucepan with about 3 inches of water and bring to a simmer. Add vinegar to the water. Put split English muffins in the toaster. Carefully break an egg in a small ramekin or cup. Slip egg into simmering water. Quickly repeat with 3 remaining eggs. Cook until whites are set but yolks are soft, about 2 to 3 minutes.

Place 2 toasted muffin halves on each plate. Top each muffin half with a slice of Canadian bacon. Use a slotted spoon to remove each egg from pan, letting excess water drip off before placing one poached egg on top of each muffin half. Divide the hollandaise sauce over the 4 muffin halves. If desired, garnish with a sprinkling of paprika or dried parsley. Serve immediately.

 I like to make this recipe with kief or hash because I think the flavor is substantially better. However, you can forego the concentrates and use 2 tablespoons cannabis-infused butter and 6 tablespoons unsalted butter instead.

Southern-Style Shrimp and Cheese Grits

Dressed up with sweet shrimp, smoky ham, sharp Cheddar cheese, and butter, these rich grits are anything but bland. The hot grits should, in theory, cook the eggs in this recipe. However, anyone with immune system compromises or concerns should play it safe and use pasteurized eggs in this recipe.

Yield: 6 cups   Serving Size: 1 cup

2 teaspoons olive oil
2 slices uncooked bacon, chopped
1/2 cup chopped green onions
1/3 pound diced ham
1 pound medium peeled raw shrimp
1/2 cup diced seeded tomatoes
4 cups water
3/4 teaspoon salt
1 cup regular grits
3 tablespoons canna-butter
6 ounces grated sharp or extra-sharp Cheddar cheese
1/2 teaspoon hot sauce, more to taste (optional)
2 large eggs
Salt and pepper to taste

Heat a large skillet over medium-high heat. Add olive oil and chopped bacon and cook until bacon begins to render fat. Add green onions and diced ham and sauté, stirring frequently, for about 5 minutes or until beginning to brown. Add shrimp and diced tomatoes to the skillet and cook, stirring often, for about 3 to 4 minutes or until shrimp are pink and not quite fully cooked. Set aside.

Bring the water and salt to a boil in a large saucepan. Whisk in grits, whisking until mixture is smooth. Reduce heat and simmer, stirring frequently, for about 10 minutes. Remove pan from heat and stir in cannabis-infused butter and grated cheese until melted and combined. Stir in hot sauce, if using. Beat eggs together and beat into grits mixture. Season to taste with salt and pepper and divide among 6 serving dishes. Top grits with shrimp/ham mixture, dividing among the 6 dishes. Serve immediately.

Freezer Friendly!
Stir the shrimp/ham mixture into the grits and place in small ramekins, cover tightly with foil, and freeze. Bake frozen ramekins in a 375-degree F oven for 40 minutes or until heated through and top is brown.

Over-Stuffed Twice-Baked Potatoes

These twice-baked stuffed potatoes are hearty enough to pair with a salad for a light meal.

Yield: 4 stuffed potato halves   Serving Size: 1 stuffed potato half

2 large russet potatoes
1 teaspoon olive oil
1/3 cup sour cream
1 gram kief or finely ground dry hash
3 slices bacon
2 green onions, white and green parts, finely chopped
1 cup shredded Cheddar cheese, divided
Salt and pepper to taste

Scrub potatoes and prick the tops with a fork. Rub potatoes with a light coating of olive oil. Bake in a 350-degree F oven for about 50 minutes or until tender when pierced with a fork. Alternately, cook potatoes in the microwave until tender.

Place sour cream in a small bowl. Sprinkle kief or finely ground dry hash over sour cream and stir to blend well. Set aside.

While potatoes are baking, heat a large skillet over medium heat. Add bacon to skillet and cook, turning once, until crisp. Drain bacon on paper towels and remove all but about 1 teaspoon bacon fat from skillet. Crumble or chop cooked bacon into small bits and set aside. Add green onions to remaining bacon fat in the skillet and sauté over medium heat for about a minute. Remove green onions from skillet with a slotted spoon and set aside.

When baked potatoes are just cool enough to handle, cut in half and scoop out the flesh into a small bowl, leaving the skin intact. Mash potatoes with sour cream/cannabis mixture using a potato masher or hand-held electric mixer. Stir in bacon bits, green onions, and 3/4 cup shredded cheese. Season to taste with salt and pepper and mix until all ingredients are well combined. Divide the mixture among the 4 hollowed-out potato skins. Divide the remaining 1/4 cup shredded cheese over the top of the 4 stuffed potatoes. Place on a baking pan and put under the broiler set on high heat just until the cheese on top melts and starts to brown, about 3 minutes. Serve hot.

Freezer Friendly!
Do not bake the second time. Cool completely, wrap in foil, and freeze. Bake frozen foil-wrapped potato at 400 degrees F for 15 minutes, reduce to 350 degrees F, and bake for about 45 minutes. Open foil during last 15 minutes.

The Ultimate Tuna Sandwich or Salad

Here's a tasty tuna salad that's equally delicious as a sandwich filling or stuffed into a hollowed-out tomato shell.

Yield: 1 cup   Serving Size: 1/2 cup

1 (6-ounce) can tuna, preferably packed in oil
1 hard-boiled egg, minced
3 tablespoons minced celery
2 tablespoons minced red or yellow onion
1 tablespoon minced parsley or cilantro

3 tablespoons mayonnaise
1 teaspoon Dijon mustard
1/4 teaspoon horseradish
1 teaspoon sweet pickle relish (optional)
1/2 gram kief or finely ground dry hash

Drain oil from tuna. In a medium bowl, combine tuna with remaining ingredients, taking care to sprinkle in the kief or ground hash in order to evenly mix. Stir until all ingredients are well combined. Serve on bread or toast for a sandwich, on a bed of lettuce for a salad, or stuffed into a large hollowed-out tomato.

Chicken and Cashew Sandwich or Salad

Chicken salad soars to new heights of flavor with this unique recipe featuring sweet red grapes, crunchy cashews, and exotic curry.

Yield: 3 cups/4 servings   Serving Size: 3/4 cup

1 gram kief or finely ground dry hash
1/2 teaspoon curry powder
1/4 cup mayonnaise
1 1/2 cups diced cooked chicken
1/2 cup halved seedless red grapes
1/4 cup finely diced celery

1 tablespoon minced onion or shallot
1/4 cup chopped cashews
1 tablespoons minced fresh Italian parsley,
    or 1 1/2 teaspoons dried
Salt and pepper to taste

Sprinkle kief or hash and curry powder over mayonnaise and mix to combine. In a medium bowl, toss remaining ingredients with mayonnaise mixture. Season to taste with salt and pepper. Serve stuffed in a pita bread, on toast, or on a bed of lettuce.

Asian-Style Steak Salad

Flame-kissed grilled steak tops a green salad dressed with a tangy lime-based dressing for an Asian-inspired main course salad.

Yield: 1/2 cup dressing/4 servings   Serving Size: 1/8 cup dressing

1 pound lean sirloin steak
Salt and pepper to taste

Dressing
2 tablespoons lime juice
1 tablespoon low-sodium soy sauce
1 1/2 teaspoons fish sauce
3/4 teaspoon sesame oil
1/2 teaspoon Sriracha hot sauce (optional)
1/2 teaspoon sugar
1/2 teaspoon minced garlic
1/4 cup neutral canna-oil

Salad
8 cups Asian salad greens blend
1/2 cup chopped cilantro
1/4 cup chopped fresh mint
8 large radishes, sliced
1 large cucumber, peeled and sliced
1 large carrot, shredded
1/4 large red onion, thinly sliced

Season steak with salt and pepper and grill over medium-high heat until rare to medium-rare. Let steak rest while you prepare the rest of the salad.

Prepare dressing by whisking together lime juice, soy sauce, fish sauce, sesame oil, Sriracha, if using, sugar, garlic, and cannabis-infused oil until mixed and emulsified.

In a large bowl, toss together salad greens, cilantro, and mint. Add dressing and toss to coat. Divide greens among 4 large chilled plates. Slice steak across the grain and arrange on top of greens. Surround edges of plate with radishes, cucumber, and carrot. Top salad with rings of red onion and serve immediately.

Store leftover dressing in the refrigerator for up to 3 days.

Easy Anytime Medicated Quesadilla

This is a quick-and-easy anytime medicated snack or meal. To get an extra-strong dose of cannabis, serve with medicated Guacamole Deluxe (page 28). Cannabis lightweights should medicate either one component or the other.

Yield: 1 quesadilla   Serving Size: 1 quesadilla

1/2 teaspoon corn or canola oil
2 corn tortillas
1/4 cup shredded Jack or pepper Jack cheese
1/4 gram kief or finely ground dry hash
Guacamole Deluxe (page 28) and your favorite salsa for serving

Heat oil in a medium skillet over medium-high heat. Place a tortilla in skillet and sprinkle the surface with shredded cheese, then sprinkle the cheese with kief or ground hash. Top with second tortilla. Heat until tortilla starts to brown and cheese starts to melt, about 2 minutes. Use a spatula to turn quesadilla over and cook until second side browns, about another 2 minutes. Remove from heat, let set for a minute before slicing. Serve with guacamole, either medicated or not depending on your preference and tolerance, and tomato salsa.

Bean and Cheese Burritos

Hearty beans combine with slightly spicy Spanish rice and creamy melted cheese for a fabulous portable vegetarian lunch. You can also customize burritos to your taste. Add cooked diced chicken, beef, pork, shrimp, fish, or tofu. Chopped grilled vegetables like onions, peppers, mushrooms, and squash also make a tasty and healthy addition.

Yield: 10 burritos   Serving Size: 1 burrito

1 tablespoon corn or vegetable oil
1/4 cup chopped onion
1 cup uncooked white or brown rice
1 1/4 cups vegetable or chicken stock
1/2 cup prepared salsa
2 1/2 grams kief or finely crumbled dry hash
10 (8-inch) flour tortillas
1 (15-ounce) can black or pinto beans, rinsed and drained
2 1/2 cups shredded Jack cheese

Heat oil in a large saucepan over medium heat. Stir in onion and cook until softened and translucent, about 5 minutes. Mix rice into pan. Cook, stirring often, until rice begins to brown, about 3 minutes. Stir in stock and salsa. Sprinkle in kief or hash and stir until dissolved. Reduce heat, cover and simmer 20 minutes, until liquid has been absorbed.

Center a tortilla on a piece of waxed paper, parchment paper, or freezer paper. Leaving about an inch margin on the bottom, layer a line of ingredients down the center: 1/4 cup beans, 1/4 cup rice, and 1/4 cup shredded cheese. Fold up the bottom of burrito, then fold one side over and roll tightly. Serve with additional salsa and hot sauce.

Freezer Friendly!
Wrap rolled burritos tightly in freezer paper or waxed paper and place in a plastic freezer bag. When ready to eat, remove from paper and place on a paper towel-lined plate. Microwave for 2 1/2 to 3 minutes or until heated through.

Easy 5-Minute Medicated Pizza Dough

Use your food processor and it only takes 5 minutes to mix up a batch of this pizza dough (extra time needed for rising, of course). You'll also find a medicated pizza sauce recipe next, use it with this dough for a strong dose, or medicate only one component for a lighter dose. This dough is dosed a little lighter than most recipes in this book.

Yield: 3 (12-inch) pizzas/6 servings   Serving Size: 1/2 pizza

1 cup very warm water (120 degrees F)
1/4 cup canna-olive oil
1 packet yeast (2 1/2 teaspoons)
2 tablespoons honey
3 1/4 cups all-purpose or bread flour

1/2 teaspoon salt
Cornmeal for dusting
Easy Pizza Sauce (see following recipe)
3 cups shredded mozzarella cheese
Assorted pizza toppings of your choice

Combine water, canna-oil, yeast, and honey in the bowl of a food processor and pulse once or twice to mix. Let rest for 2 or 3 minutes or until small bubbles start to form. Add flour and salt and turn on the food processor. In a minute or so a ball of dough will start to form. If dough seems too wet, add a little extra flour, but know that too wet is better than too dry, and the dough will lose some of the stickiness as it rises. Alternately, use an electric stand mixer fitted with a dough hook to mix the dough.

Pour about a teaspoon of olive oil into the bottom of a large bowl and put a little on your hands. Remove dough from food processor or mixer and form into a ball. Place ball in bowl and turn to lightly coat with oil. Cover with a clean kitchen towel and place in a warm, draft-free place to rise for about 1 hour or until doubled in size.

Preheat oven to 475 degrees F. Place a baking stone in the oven. (If you don't have a baking stone, use a pizza pan.)

Divide dough ball into 3 pieces. Roll out each piece into a 12-inch circle on a lightly floured surface. Lightly sprinkle pizza peel and baking stone with cornmeal. If you are using a pizza pan instead, lightly oil the pan with olive oil. Place dough on pizza peel or in pan. Spread a layer of sauce on top with 1 cup shredded mozzarella cheese. Add pizza toppings to your liking such as pepperoni, sausage, onions, bell peppers, mushrooms, etc. Slide pizza onto baking stone or place pan in oven and bake until crust is browned and cheese is melted, 12 to 15 minutes. Remove pizza from oven and cool on a wire rack for 5 minutes before slicing. Get next pizza rolled and ready to top while previous pizza is baking.

Freezer Friendly!
Freeze extra unbaked dough, lightly coated with olive oil, in a plastic freezer bag. Bring to room temperature (thaw either in the fridge or countertop) before rolling and baking as above.

Easy Pizza Sauce

This delicious pizza sauce requires no cooking and goes together in a snap. If your pizza dough is medicated, you may want to leave cannabis out of the sauce or vice-versa unless you are looking for an extra-strong dosed edible.

Yield: 1 1/2 cups   Serving Size: 1/4 cup

1 (4-ounce) can tomato paste
4 ounces water
1/4 cup canna-olive oil
3/4 teaspoon minced garlic
3/4 teaspoon marjoram
1 teaspoon dried oregano
1 teaspoon dried basil
1/2 teaspoon crushed red pepper, more to taste (optional)
1 teaspoon balsamic vinegar

In a medium bowl, whisk together all ingredients until well combined. Let stand for several hours before using to allow the flavors to mingle. Spread a thin layer of sauce on pizza dough before topping with cheese and desired pizza toppings and baking.

 Freezer Friendly!
Freeze leftover pizza sauce in a lidded freezer container. Simply thaw and use.

New Orleans-Style Muffuletta Sandwich

While tourists may think of Po' Boys, New Orleans natives know the Crescent City's favorite sandwich is really the Muffuletta – a round loaf of crusty bread over stuffed with ham, salami, provolone and an unforgettable briny olive salad. The medicated olive salad portion of this recipe is a versatile ingredient that can also be used to season pastas, steamed vegetables, and grilled meat dishes.

Yield: 1 1/2 cups olive spread/1 (8- to 10-inch) sandwich
Serving Size: 1/4 cup olive spread (1/6 sandwich)

Olive Salad
1/3 cup brine-cured black olives,
   such as kalamatas
1/4 cup green olives
1/2 cup finely chopped celery, with leaves
1/2 cup Giardiniera (Italian pickled vegetables)
1/4 cup chopped fresh Italian parsley
1 teaspoon minced garlic
1/4 cup canna-olive oil
1/2 teaspoon freshly ground black pepper
1/2 teaspoon crushed red pepper (optional)

Sandwich
1 (8- to 10-inch) round loaf of crusty bread
6 ounces sliced Provolone cheese
6 ounces sliced smoked ham
3 ounces sliced Genoa salami
2 medium ripe tomatoes, sliced
1/2 small onion, thinly sliced

     Pit olives (if necessary) and combine with celery, Giardiniera, Italian parsley, garlic, canna-oil, black pepper, and crushed red pepper (if using) in the bowl of a food processor. Process until mixed, but still somewhat chunky—do not purée.

     Cut the bread horizontally in half. Remove some of the soft center to allow room for the filling (use bread centers for another purpose). Spread half the olive salad on the bottom of the bread. Follow with a layer of cheese, followed by layers of ham, salami, tomatoes, and onion. Finish off with another layer of cheese and the remaining olive salad. Wrap sandwich tightly in foil and refrigerate for at least 3 hours before serving (you can make this a day ahead of time and it will still be great). Let stand at room temperature for about 30 minutes before serving. Cut into 6 wedges to serve.

Freezer Friendly!
Freeze extra olive salad in a lidded container. You can also freeze extra portions of tightly wrapped Muffuletta sandwiches, minus the tomato and onion. In both cases, thaw in the fridge and enjoy.

Stuffed Open-Face Sandwich Melts

Sweet onions and peppers mix with meaty mushrooms and ground beef, and creamy melted cheese brings it all together in a sandwich hearty enough to satisfy big appetites.

Yield: 2 open-face sandwiches/4 servings   Serving Size: 1/2 of 1 sandwich

2 grams kief or finely crumbled dry hash
1/3 cup mayonnaise
2 teaspoons olive oil, divided
3/4 pound lean ground beef
4 ounces sliced mushrooms
1 medium bell pepper, finely diced
1 medium onion, finely diced
3 garlic cloves, minced
1 1/2 teaspoons soy sauce
1 1/2 teaspoons Worcestershire sauce
1 cup grated Provolone cheese
Salt and pepper to taste
1/4 teaspoon cayenne pepper, more to taste (optional)
1 (1-pound) loaf French bread

In a small bowl, sprinkle kief or finely crumbled dry hash into mayonnaise. Stir to evenly combine cannabis into mayonnaise. Set aside.

Heat 1 teaspoon olive oil in a large skillet over medium-high heat. Add ground beef and cook, stirring constantly to break up chunks into small pieces, until just cooked through, about 6 to 7 minutes. Remove from pan, drain meat in a colander to remove any excess fat. Place cooked meat in a large bowl. Add remaining teaspoon olive oil to the same skillet. Add diced pepper and onion and cook, stirring frequently, until softened and beginning to brown, about 5 minutes. Add garlic to pan and stir; cook for 2 minutes, then remove to colander to drain.

In a large bowl, mix drained cooked vegetables with ground beef. Toss meat mixture with grated cheese and mayonnaise mixture and stir until well combined. Season to taste with salt and pepper and cayenne, if using.

Preheat the oven to 350 degrees F. Cut bread loaf in half lengthwise. Remove some of the inner bread to make a hollowed-out shell. Divide the filling mixture between the 2 hollow bread shells. Bake for about 15 minutes or until cheese is melted and filling is heated through.

Freezer Friendly!
If you don't want to make both sandwiches at once, package the filling in a plastic freezer bag or lidded freezer container. Thaw in the fridge, then continue with filling and baking instructions above.

Roast Beef Roll-Ups 33

Hummus 30

Argentine-Style Empanadas 41

Asian Shrimp Salad Rolls 37

Crab Rangoon 35

Gougères 40

Herbed Yeast Dinner Rolls 122

Deviled Eggs 32

French Onion Soup au Gratin 47

Roasted Garlic and Onion Soup 46

Gazpacho 44

Almost Caesar Salad 53

Fruit Salad Stuffed Cantaloupe 52

Wedge Salad with Blue Cheese Dressing 52

Southern Sweet Potato Casserole 118

Sliders 42

Cranberry Applesauce Bread 64

Easy 5-Minute Medicated Pizza Dough 77   *Easy Pizza Sauce 78*

New Orleans "Barbecue" Shrimp 100

Stir-Fried Ginger Shrimp and Asparagus 102

Beef Stroganoff 108

Cornish Game Hens with Peach, Sausage, and Rice Stuffing 107

Chicken Pot Pies with Puff Pastry Crust 106

Strawberry Licuado 128

Peaches and Cream Smoothie 127

Devilishly Good Orange Smoothie 126

Piña Colada Smoothie 127

Mini Pineapple Upside-Down Cakes 142

Snickerdoodles 147

Toffee Chocolate Chip Cookies 146

Red Velvet Cupcakes with Cream Cheese Icing 144

Molten Chocolate Lava Cakes 140

Main Courses

While it can sometimes seem challenging to find main courses that work well for cannabis cooking, there are a lot of possibilities. Sure, the plain and simple grilled proteins won't work, but many sauces regularly served with them will. A good medicated sauce like the pesto or barbecue sauces at the end of this chapter can instantly medicate all kinds of foods.

Other entrées contain enough butter or oil to give a serving a sufficient cannabis dose when using marijuana butter and oil infusions, but exercise some caution here. Take care to avoid high-temperature cooking methods with your butter or oil, such as sautéing or frying, or you will render the THC in it useless (review Chapter 1 as to why). You can bake or roast at higher temperatures because the food itself will not reach the temperature in the oven, but always take care when exposing cannabis butter or oil to direct heat.

As always, if you have access to kief or hash you can add cannabis to almost any recipe.

Vegetable Lasagna

Meaty eggplant and mushrooms provide substance in this vegetarian version of the classic pasta dish.

Yield: 1 (8-inch square) pan   Serving Size: 1/4 of 1 pan

1/2 pound lasagna noodles
Salt to taste
1 medium eggplant
6 tablespoons olive oil, divided
3 1/2 teaspoons minced garlic, divided
3 medium zucchini, cut into lengthwise planks
Pepper to taste
4 ounces sliced white or cremini mushrooms
1 small onion, peeled and diced
1 medium bell pepper, cored, seeded and diced
1 (28-ounce) can crushed tomatoes,
    plus juices

1/2 (6-ounce) can tomato paste
1 tablespoon balsamic vinegar
1 bay leaf
1 tablespoon Italian seasoning
2 grams finely ground cannabis bud
1/4 teaspoon crushed red pepper, more to taste
    (optional)
2 large eggs
16 ounces whole milk ricotta cheese
1/2 cup grated Parmesan cheese
2 tablespoons minced fresh Italian parsley
4 ounces grated mozzarella cheese

Cook pasta in a large pot of boiling salted water until flexible, but not quite cooked through. Drain, rinse, and keep moist in a pot of cold water until needed.

Preheat oven to 375 degrees F. Cut the ends off eggplant and slice into 1/2-inch slices. Coat eggplant slices liberally with salt and set aside for 15 minutes.

Combine 1/4 cup olive oil with 2 teaspoons garlic. Rinse salt off eggplant and pat dry with paper towels. Brush sliced eggplant and zucchini planks liberally with garlic oil and season with salt and pepper. Spray 2 large baking sheets with cooking spray. Place eggplant and zucchini on the sheets in a single layer and roast for about 20 minutes. Turn vegetables over and roast for another 20 minutes or until browned. Maintain oven temperature.

In a large saucepan oven over medium heat, heat 1 tablespoon olive oil. Add mushrooms and onion and sauté for about 5 minutes. Add pepper and remaining 1 1/2 teaspoons garlic and sauté for another 5 minutes. Add tomatoes and their juices. Stir in tomato paste, balsamic vinegar, bay leaf, Italian seasoning, and crushed red pepper (if using). Increase heat, bring to a boil, lower heat, cover, and simmer, stirring often, for 15 minutes. Stir in ground cannabis bud and cook for about 3 more minutes. Remove from heat and remove bay leaf.

Beat eggs until frothy. Stir beaten eggs together with ricotta, Parmesan, and parsley.

Spoon a thin layer of tomato sauce on the bottom of an 8-inch baking pan. Arrange a layer of noodles to cover the bottom of the pan, overlapping as necessary for fit. Add a layer of eggplant, a layer of zucchini, a layer of the ricotta mixture, and a sprinkling of mozzarella. Cover with tomato sauce. Repeat the layering process. End with a layer of pasta, cover with sauce, and sprinkle with remaining mozzarella on top. Bake for about 40 minutes or until bubbling.

 Freezer Friendly!
Cool leftovers, cover tightly with foil, and freeze. Place uncovered lasagna in a 375-degree F oven until heated through, cheese has melted and browned on top, and sauce is bubbling. Timing will depend on portion size.

Chiles Rellenos

Fresh green poblano or Anaheim chiles are stuffed with tangy Jack cheese and seasoned with a sprinkling of kief or hash before being batter-coated and fried. Add a pool of spicy enchilada sauce, and you have the ultimate stuffed peppers.

Yield: 6 chile rellenos   Serving Size: 1 chile relleno

6 large fresh poblano or Anaheim chiles
1 1/2 grams kief or finely ground dry hash
9 ounces Jack cheese
1/2 cup plus 1 tablespoon all-purpose flour
1 1/2 cups red or green canned or
    homemade enchilada sauce
6 eggs, separated
1 teaspoon salt
1 cup vegetable, canola, or corn oil for frying

   Preheat the broiler. Place chiles on a foil-covered pan and roast close to the broiler element, turning frequently, until most of the surface is blackened. Alternately, blacken chiles directly on the grate of a gas stove over a high flame or over a very hot grill fire. Place hot blackened chiles in a brown paper bag and immediately fold closed so chiles steam. Let rest for 15 minutes.
   Remove chiles from bag and carefully peel off the skin. Rinse chiles. Carefully cut a lengthwise slit starting just below stem and going almost to the bottom. Reach inside and carefully remove as much of the inner membranes and seeds as possible while keeping the pepper intact. Pat chiles dry and lay out on a parchment- or foil-covered baking sheet. Sprinkle 1/4 gram kief or finely ground hash into each chile, making a thin line inside from close to the stem to almost the bottom of the pepper. Carefully stuff each pepper, over the kief or hash, with about 1 1/2 ounces shredded cheese. Adjust the amount of cheese to the size of your peppers; do not stuff so full the slit won't close. Place 1/2 cup flour on a large plate. Dredge each stuffed chile in the flour until all sides are lightly coated. Return to baking sheet and set aside.
   Heat enchilada sauce in the microwave or in a small saucepan on the stove and keep warm.
   Beat the egg whites in a small bowl until stiff peaks form. In a separate medium bowl, beat egg yolks and remaining 1 tablespoon flour and 1 teaspoon salt. Stir beaten egg whites into yolk mixture until combined and a thick paste forms.
   Heat oil in a large skillet, wok, or deep fryer until hot but not smoking, about 370 degrees F. Working in batches, dip each chile in the batter and place in the hot oil, slit side down. Cook for about 1 1/2 to 2 minutes or until golden brown. Turn and cook second side for another minute or so or until browned. Drain on a wire rack while you divide the enchilada sauce among 6 plates. Place a hot stuffed pepper over sauce and serve immediately.

New Orleans "Barbecue" Shrimp

I'm not sure how this famous New Orleans recipe came to be known as "barbecue," as there is no grill, fire, or smoking involved. Nonetheless, its intensely flavored, herb-laden sauce is delicious. Serve with plenty of crusty bread for soaking up every drop.

Yield: 1 cup broth plus shrimp   Serving Size: 1/2 cup broth plus shrimp

2 tablespoons canna-butter
6 tablespoons unsalted butter
1 tablespoon crushed garlic
2 tablespoons Worcestershire sauce
1 tablespoon lemon juice
1/2 cup beer
1 1/2 teaspoons dried rosemary
1 1/2 teaspoons dried oregano
1 1/2 teaspoons dried thyme
1 teaspoon dried basil
1/2 teaspoon black pepper
3/4 pound unpeeled large raw shrimp, heads removed
Crusty bread for serving

Melt canna-butter and butter in a large skillet over medium heat. Add garlic, Worcestershire sauce, lemon juice, beer, rosemary, oregano, thyme, basil, and pepper and heat to bubbling. Add shrimp to skillet and cook, stirring and turning shrimp occasionally, until shrimp are pink and cooked through, about 5 minutes. Divide broth and shrimp between two bowls and serve with plenty of crusty bread.

Fettuccine Alfredo

Rich, creamy, and cheesy Alfredo sauce is an indulgent addition to any meal. Spoon over hot cooked pasta for instant dinner. Or use to adorn simple grilled or steamed chicken, fish, or vegetables.

Yield: 3 cups sauce plus pasta   Serving Size: 1/2 cup sauce plus pasta

1 1/2 pounds fresh or dried fettuccine
6 tablespoons canna-butter
6 tablespoons unsalted butter
1 tablespoon minced garlic
2 cups half-and-half
1 teaspoon pepper or white pepper
3/4 cup (3 ounces) grated Parmesan cheese
1 cup (4 ounces) grated whole milk mozzarella cheese
Salt and additional pepper to taste

Cook fettuccine according to package directions. Drain.

Melt the canna-butter and butter in a large saucepan over medium-low heat. Add the garlic and cook, stirring, for 30 seconds. Add the half-and-half and pepper. Bring to a simmer, stirring frequently and watching carefully to prevent pot from boiling over, which can happen quickly. Stir in Parmesan and cook, stirring constantly, for 5 minutes. Stir in mozzarella and continue to cook until cheese melts, about 5 minutes. Remove from heat and whisk or use an immersion blender to smooth sauce. Pour over hot cooked pasta and serve.

Freezer Friendly!
Freeze cooled extra sauce in a lidded container. Defrost in the refrigerator and reheat in a saucepan on the stovetop over medium-low heat. If mixture separates, whisk vigorously to make everything good as new.

Stir-Fried Ginger Shrimp and Asparagus

This satisfying stir-fry dinner goes together in a flash. Serve over rice or your favorite Asian-style noodles.

Yield: 4 cups   Serving Size: 1 cup plus rice or noodles

1/2 teaspoon minced garlic
2 tablespoons minced fresh ginger
1/3 cup chicken or vegetable stock
2 tablespoons rice vinegar
2 tablespoons oyster sauce
1 tablespoon sesame oil
1 teaspoon sugar
1/2 teaspoon black pepper
2 teaspoons cornstarch
3 tablespoons melted canna-butter
4 teaspoons vegetable or canola oil, divided
1 pound peeled fresh medium raw shrimp
2 cups fresh trimmed asparagus pieces
   (cut each stalk into 4 to 5 pieces)
4 ounces sliced white, cremini, or shiitake mushrooms
4 green onions, white and green parts, minced

Whisk together garlic, ginger, stock, vinegar, oyster sauce, sesame oil, sugar, pepper, and cornstarch until well combined. Whisk in melted cannabis-infused butter until well combined and mixture is emulsified. You can alternately prepare sauce in a small food processor. Set aside.

Heat a wok over high heat. Add 2 teaspoons oil and swirl to coat wok. Add shrimp and stir-fry just until cooked, about 4 to 5 minutes. Remove shrimp from wok and set aside. Add remaining 2 teaspoons oil to wok and swirl to coat. Add asparagus, mushrooms, and green onions to wok and stir-fry until crisp-tender, about 6 minutes. Return shrimp to wok and stir to combine ingredients. Stir sauce and pour over ingredients in wok. Cook, stirring constantly, for about a minute or until sauce heats through, thickens, and evenly coats the food. Serve immediately over rice or noodles.

 Oyster sauce, a staple of Chinese cuisine, is a thick, dark brown sauce made from ground dried oysters. Available at Asian food markets or well stocked grocery stores, oyster sauce will keep indefinitely in your refrigerator.

Lobster Newburg

Sweet lobster is encased in a creamy, sherry-flavored Newburg sauce for an indulgent special occasion entrée.

Yield: 4 1/2 cups/6 servings   Serving Size: 3/4 cup

3 tablespoons unsalted butter
1 medium shallot, peeled and minced
2 tablespoons all-purpose flour
1 1/2 grams kief or finely ground dry hash
1 1/4 cups half-and-half
1/4 teaspoon grated nutmeg
1/8 teaspoon cayenne, more to taste (optional)
Salt and pepper to taste
1 large egg yolk
3 tablespoons dry sherry or white wine
2 1/2 cups cooked chopped lobster meat
6 pieces toast, or 6 baked puff pastry shells for serving

Melt butter in a medium saucepan over medium heat. Add shallot and cook, stirring, until softened, about 2 minutes. Sprinkle with flour and kief or hash and stir with a whisk to combine. Whisk in the half-and-half until smooth. Whisk in nutmeg and cayenne, if using. Season to taste with salt and pepper.

In a separate small bowl, whisk together egg yolk and sherry or white wine. Rapidly whisk sherry mixture into saucepan and bring to a simmer, stirring constantly. Remove from heat and stir cooked seafood into sauce. Spoon sauce over hot pieces of toast or into baked puff pastry shells and serve immediately.

 Find frozen, ready-to-bake puff pastry shells in the freezer section of your favorite supermarket.

Chicken or Tofu Green Chile Enchiladas

Enjoy comfort food south-of-the-border–style with cheesy chicken or tofu, bean, and corn-stuffed enchiladas smothered in a spiced green chile sauce.

Yield: 8 enchiladas   Serving Size: 2 enchiladas

3/4 gram kief or finely ground dry hash
1/2 cup sour cream or low-fat sour cream
1 1/2 cups cooked diced chicken, or 1 1/2 cups
  cubed drained firm or extra-firm tofu
1/2 cup cooked black beans
2 (4-ounce) cans diced green chiles, divided
1/2 cup fresh, frozen, or canned corn, drained
1 1/2 cups grated Monterey Jack
  cheese, divided

1/2 teaspoon ground cumin
1/2 teaspoon dried oregano
1/2 teaspoon garlic powder
1 teaspoon chili powder
Salt and pepper to taste
8 (8-inch) corn or flour tortillas
1 (28-ounce) can green enchilada sauce

Preheat oven to 350 degrees F. In a small bowl, sprinkle kief or ground dry hash over sour cream and stir until cannabis is evenly distributed in the sour cream. In a large bowl, combine the diced chicken or tofu, sour cream mixture, black beans, 1 can green chiles, corn, 1 cup grated cheese, cumin, oregano, garlic powder, and chili powder. Add salt and pepper to taste and toss to mix all the ingredients together.

Place a tortilla on a clean surface. Place 1/2 cup filling mixture down the center and roll the tortilla. Place seam side down in a baking dish that has been sprayed with cooking spray. Repeat with remaining tortillas and filling, placing enchiladas with sides touching to completely fill the baking pan.

Stir remaining can green chiles with enchilada sauce to mix well. Pour sauce over prepared enchiladas. Sprinkle with remaining 1/2 cup grated cheese. Bake for about 30 minutes or until heated through and cheese on top has melted and browned. Serve hot.

Freezer Friendly!
Cover extra unbaked portions with foil and freeze. Bake uncovered frozen pan at 375 degrees F until heated through—about 45 minutes for a 2-enchilada portion. Use flour tortillas for freezing as corn tortillas turn mushy.

Chicken Curry

A ginger and curry-spiced yogurt sauce surrounds tender pieces of white meat chicken. Serve over fragrant jasmine or basmati rice.

Yield: 4 cups plus rice   Serving Size: 1 cup plus rice

2 grams kief or finely crumbled dry hash
1/2 cup plain yogurt (NOT low-fat or fat-free)
2 tablespoons vegetable or olive oil
2 pounds boneless skinless chicken breasts,
    cut into 1-inch cubes
1 large onion, diced
1 jalapeño pepper, cored, seeded and minced
2 teaspoons grated fresh ginger
1 1/2 teaspoons minced garlic
1 tablespoon curry powder
1/2 teaspoon turmeric
1/2 cup water
1/4 cup minced cilantro
Salt and pepper to taste
Cooked rice for serving

Sprinkle kief or finely crumbled hash into yogurt. Stir to combine and dissolve the cannabis into the yogurt. Set aside while you prepare the rest of the dish.

Heat oil in a large skillet over medium-high heat. Add chicken, onion, and jalapeño and cook, stirring frequently with a wooden spoon, until chicken is beginning to brown and onion is softened and translucent, about 5 minutes. Stir in ginger, garlic, curry powder, and turmeric and mix until well combined. Reduce heat to medium-low. Stir in yogurt mixture and cook, stirring constantly, until thickened, about 3 minutes. Stir in water and cilantro. Season to taste with salt and pepper. Reduce heat to low and cover. Simmer, stirring occasionally, for about 15 minutes or until chicken is cooked through. Serve over cooked rice.

Freezer Friendly!
Top cooled cooked rice with cooled curry in a lidded freezer container. When ready to eat, microwave frozen on High, stopping to stir every minute or so, until heated through.

Chicken Pot Pies with Puff Pastry Crust

Chicken along with crunchy carrots, celery, and sweet green peas nestle together in a creamy sauce under a flaky puff pastry crust for a comfort food classic. You can substitute cooked turkey for chicken, making for a tasty way to use up Thanksgiving leftovers.

Yield: 6 cups   Serving Size: 1 cup plus crust

2 tablespoons olive oil
3 medium carrots, peeled and finely diced
3 medium celery ribs, finely diced
1 large onion, finely diced
1 1/2 teaspoons minced garlic
3/4 cup frozen or canned green peas
1/4 cup minced fresh Italian parsley
3/4 teaspoon ground dried sage
1/2 teaspoon dried thyme

3 tablespoons unsalted butter
1/3 cup all-purpose flour
1 1/2 cups chicken stock
1 cup whole milk
1 1/2 grams kief or hash
2 cups diced cooked chicken
Salt and pepper to taste
1/2 (17-ounce) package or 1 sheet frozen
   puff pastry, thawed

Preheat oven to 400 degrees F. Heat olive oil in a large skillet over medium-high heat. Add carrots, celery, onion, and garlic and cook, stirring frequently, until softened, about 5 minutes. Stir in peas, parsley, sage, and thyme. Stir until well combined. Remove from heat.

Melt the butter in a large saucepan over medium heat. Whisk in the flour until smooth. Cook, whisking constantly, for 1 minute. Whisk in chicken stock and milk until smooth. Continue to cook, stirring constantly with a wooden spoon, until mixture comes to a simmer. Sprinkle in kief or hash and cook, stirring, for another 2 minutes until cannabis concentrate has dissolved and sauce has slightly thickened. Stir in cooked chicken and prepared vegetables. Season to taste with salt and pepper.

Spray 6 ramekins, or baking dishes large enough to hold 1 cup filling and crust, with cooking spray. Divide filling mixture among them, filling each about 2/3 full.

Follow directions on puff pastry box for thawing and rolling. Use a sharp knife to cut prepared pastry to the size of the top of the baking dishes and set on top of chicken mixture. Bake until crust is puffed and brown and filling is bubbly, about 18 to 20 minutes.

Freezer Friendly!
Cool filling and defrost dough just until flexible enough to handle and cut. Place dough on top of baking dishes of cooled filling, cover tightly, and freeze. Bake frozen pies uncovered at 400 degrees F for 30 minutes or until bubbly.

Cornish Game Hens with Peach, Sausage, and Rice Stuffing

This main course is elegant enough to serve for a fancy holiday dinner where everyone gets their own individual bird stuffed with orange-scented rice stuffing studded with spicy sausage and sweet peaches. Or use the stuffing to stuff 2 small roasting chickens or 1 small turkey. You can make the stuffing portion of this recipe a day or two ahead of time and store in a plastic storage bag in the fridge until ready for use.

Yield: 4 stuffed hens   Serving Size: 1 stuffed hen

1 cup chicken stock
1/2 cup orange juice, divided
2 teaspoons orange zest
1 tablespoon butter
3/4 cup jasmine or basmati brown rice
1 1/2 grams kief or finely ground dry hash
1 tablespoon olive oil

6 ounces low-fat pork sausage
1/2 medium onion, diced
3/4 cup diced fresh, frozen, or canned peaches
1/4 teaspoon hot sauce, more to taste
4 Rock Cornish game hens
1/2 cup peach or apricot preserves
Salt and pepper to taste

Bring chicken stock, 1/4 cup orange juice, orange zest, and 1 tablespoon butter to a boil in a medium saucepan over medium-high heat. Stir in rice, reduce heat to a low simmer, cover, and cook until done, about 20 minutes. When rice is cooked, open lid and sprinkle kief or ground hash over rice, stir well to evenly combine cannabis into rice.

Heat 1 tablespoon olive oil in a large skillet. Add crumbled sausage and onion and sauté over medium heat until sausage is cooked and onion begins to brown, about 6 to 8 minutes. Add diced peaches and hot sauce and stir to mix. Stir in cooked rice mixture and season to taste with salt, pepper, and additional hot sauce, if needed.

Preheat oven to 375 degrees F. Prepare glaze by mixing together remaining 1/4 cup orange juice and peach or apricot preserves in a small bowl. Set aside.

If necessary, remove the neck and giblets from the game hens and discard or reserve for another purpose. Wash hens inside and out with cold water and pat dry with paper towels. Spray a large baking dish with cooking spray. Loosely stuff each bird with about 3/4 cup stuffing. Truss the bird by running a length of kitchen twine under the bird, bringing it up to hold the wings in, crossing the twine over itself across the breast and around the drumsticks, then tying in a knot across the breast (This step isn't essential, but does keep everything neat and pretty.)

Brush the outside of the stuffed hens lightly with olive oil and season with salt and pepper. Bake for 30 minutes. Brush hens with glaze, return to oven, and bake for 15 minutes more. Let rest for 5 to 10 minutes before serving.

 Freezer Friendly!
Freeze extra unbaked stuffing in a lidded container or plastic freezer bag. When ready to use, thaw in the refrigerator before stuffing hens and proceeding as above.

Beef Stroganoff

An old-fashioned favorite that still tastes great today, creamy sauced noodles and beef make a satisfying dinner.

Yield: 8 cups noodles and sauce   Serving Size: 2 cups

1/2 cup sour cream
1 gram kief or finely ground dry hash
1 pound wide egg noodles
3 tablespoons unsalted butter, divided
2 tablespoons all-purpose flour
2 cups beef stock
2 teaspoons Dijon mustard
Salt and pepper to taste
1 tablespoon olive oil
1 medium onion, diced
8 ounces sliced mushrooms
1 teaspoon minced garlic
1 1/2 pounds thinly sliced beef sirloin
2 tablespoons finely chopped fresh
   Italian parsley for garnish

   In a small bowl, combine sour cream with kief or ground dry hash until evenly combined. Set aside. Cook noodles according to package directions. Drain and set aside.
   Heat a large saucepan over medium heat. Melt 2 tablespoons butter before stirring in the flour, cooking and stirring constantly for 1 minute. Whisk in the beef stock. Cook, stirring constantly, for about 2 minutes. Reduce heat to low. Stir in mustard and sour cream/cannabis mixture until smooth and then cook, stirring for another minute. Remove from heat and season to taste with salt and pepper.
   Heat a large skillet over medium-high heat. Add 1 tablespoon olive oil and remaining tablespoon of butter. When butter melts, add onion and mushrooms and cook until browned, about 5 to 6 minutes. Add garlic and sliced beef and cook, stirring, until beef is browned, 3 to 4 minutes.
   In a large bowl, toss cooked noodles with meat mixture and sauce until well combined. Season to taste with salt and pepper. Divide among 4 plates and garnish with chopped parsley. Serve immediately.

Better-Than-Mom's Meat Loaf

Kicked up with spicy jalapeños (and cannabis, of course) and coated in a sweet-and-spicy glaze, this is not your mother's meat loaf. Substitute all or part of the beef or pork for ground buffalo or ground turkey for a lower fat meat loaf.

Yield: 3 (3 3/4 x 6 1/2-inch) loaves/6 servings　　Serving Size: 1/2 of 1 loaf, or 1/6 of recipe

Meat Loaf
1 1/2 pounds 85% lean ground beef
1 pound ground pork
1 1/2 grams kief or finely ground dry hash,
　or 3 grams finely ground bud
2 teaspoons minced garlic
1 or 2 jalapeño peppers, cored, seeded,
　and minced
1 medium white or yellow onion,
　finely chopped
1 teaspoon dried thyme
1 teaspoon dried oregano

1 1/2 teaspoons salt
1 1/2 teaspoons pepper
3/4 cup dry bread crumbs
1 large egg

Glaze
1/3 cup ketchup
1 tablespoon Worcestershire sauce
1/2 teaspoon soy sauce
1 teaspoon chili powder
Hot sauce to taste

Preheat oven to 325 degrees F. Line a large baking sheet with parchment paper or spray liberally with cooking spray.

Place ground beef and pork in a large bowl. Sprinkle the kief, hash, or ground bud over the meat and use clean hands to thoroughly mix the cannabis into the meat. Add the garlic, jalapeño, onion, thyme, oregano, salt, pepper, bread crumbs, and egg and continue to mix until all ingredients are evenly combined. While I tested the recipe using a small (3 3/4 × 6 1/2-inch) loaf pan, you can make the loaf any size you like. Just keep in mind a single dose serving is 1/6 of the total recipe. Use a loaf pan to help mold a third of the meat into a loaf shape, then carefully remove from the pan and place the loaf on the prepared baking pan. Repeat with the remaining meat to make two more loaves. Bake for 15 minutes.

In the meantime, prepare the glaze by mixing together ketchup, Worcestershire sauce, soy sauce, chili powder, and hot sauce until blended. Use a pastry brush to brush on the tops and sides of meat loaf. Continue to bake until cooked though and browned on top, about 40 more minutes.

Freezer Friendly!
Wrap leftover baked meat loaf tightly in foil and freeze. Thaw in the fridge and it's ready to eat cold. Alternately, warm in the microwave or in a 375-degree F oven for about 40 minutes or until heated through.

Medicated Meatballs in Marinara

Classic Italian tomato sauce envelops savory meatballs that can be enjoyed over spaghetti or on an Italian roll with melted cheese for a hot meatball submarine sandwich.

Yield: 6 cups meatballs and sauce   Serving Size: 1 cup

Meatballs
1/2 pound ground pork
1/2 pound lean ground beef
1/2 small onion, diced
1 tablespoon minced garlic
1 large egg
1/4 cup dry bread crumbs
2 tablespoons chopped fresh Italian
   parsley, or 1 tablespoon dried parsley
3/4 teaspoon salt
1/2 teaspoon pepper
1 1/2 grams kief or finely crumbled dry hash,
   or 3 grams finely ground bud
1 tablespoon olive oil for sautéeing

Sauce
2 tablespoons olive oil
1 small onion, diced
2 teaspoons minced garlic
1 (28-ounce) can plum tomatoes plus juices
2 tablespoons tomato paste
1 bay leaf
2 teaspoons Italian seasoning
1/2 teaspoon crushed red pepper (optional)
Salt and pepper to taste

In a large bowl combine ground pork, ground beef, 1/2 small diced onion, 1 tablespoon minced garlic, egg, bread crumbs, Italian parsley, salt, pepper and kief, hash, or ground bud. Use your hands to mix until everything is well combined. Roll mixture into small balls about 2 tablespoons each.

Heat 1 tablespoon olive oil in a large skillet over medium-low heat. Sauté meatballs for about 5 to 6 minutes, turning to brown on all sides, until just browned but not quite cooked through. Remove from pan with a slotted spoon and drain any excess fat.

Heat 2 tablespoons olive oil in a large saucepan over medium heat. Add onion and garlic and cook, stirring frequently, until soft, about 3 minutes. Purée tomatoes and their juices in a food processor along with the tomato paste. Stir tomato mixture into pan. Add bay leaf, Italian seasoning, and crushed red pepper (if using). Season to taste with salt and pepper. Bring to a simmer, add meatballs to the sauce, and simmer for about 12 minutes until meatballs are cooked through and sauce is thickened. Serve heated meatballs and sauce over cooked spaghetti, or spoon into a split Italian roll, top with mozzarella cheese, and cook under the broiler until cheese melts for a Hot Meatball Sub.

Freezer Friendly!
Cool completely, then package in a freezer bag. To reheat, microwave, thawed or frozen, just until heated, or heat thawed meatballs and marinara on stovetop over medium-low heat, stirring frequently, until heated through.

Apple and Cornbread-Stuffed Pork Chops

What could be better than juicy pork chops stuffed with corn bread, tart apples, and smoky bacon?

Yield: 2 stuffed pork chops   Serving Size: 1 stuffed pork chop

1/2 cup chicken stock
1/2 gram kief or hash
1 slice bacon
1/2 small onion, finely diced
1 small Granny Smith apple, peeled,
   cored, and finely diced

1 cup dried corn bread cubes
3 tablespoons minced fresh Italian parsley,
   or 1 tablespoon dried
Salt and pepper to taste
2 bone-in rib or loin pork chops,
   1 1/4-inches thick

Preheat oven to 350 degrees F. Place chicken stock in a small pan over low heat. Stir in kief or hash and cook, stirring, until dissolved. Set aside.

Cut the slice of bacon into small pieces and cook in a medium skillet over medium heat, stirring occasionally, until crisp. Add onion to the skillet with the bacon and cook for 2 to 3 minutes or until softened and starting to brown. Remove from heat and stir in apple, corn bread cubes, and parsley. Add chicken stock/cannabis mixture and salt and pepper to taste and mix until everything is well combined. Make a pocket in each pork chop by cutting through the meat toward the bone. Fill each pocket with the stuffing. Spray a baking pan with cooking spray, place stuffed chops in the pan, and bake, uncovered, for about 45 minutes or until chops are browned and meat is cooked through. Let rest for 5 minutes before serving.

Pesto Sauce

With strong flavor components like fresh basil, garlic, olive oil, and Parmesan cheese, you'll never notice the taste of the cannabis-infused oil in this recipe. Serve versatile pesto sauce with pasta or over steamed or grilled vegetables, chicken, fish, or tofu for an instant meal. You can even use a light coating of pesto instead of sauce on pizza. Using all canna-oil in this recipe will yield a strong per-serving dose. If you want a lighter dosed pesto, substitute some of the canna-oil for regular olive oil.

Yield: 1 cup pesto/8 servings   Serving Size: 2 tablespoons

1 cup loosely packed fresh basil
3/4 teaspoon minced garlic
1/2 cup freshly grated Parmesan cheese

1/4 cup toasted pine nuts or walnuts
1/2 cup canna-olive oil (see note above)
Salt and pepper to taste

In the bowl of a food processor or blender combine basil, garlic, Parmesan, and pine nuts or walnuts. Process to mix. With machine running, slowly drizzle in canna-olive oil and regular olive oil, if using. Season to taste with salt and pepper.

Freezer Friendly!
Freeze extra pesto sauce in a lidded container. Simply thaw and use.

Barbecue Sauce for Grilled Meats

While not an entrée in its own right, just add this sweet-and-spicy barbecue sauce to your favorite kind of grilled meat for instant dinner. If you like your sauce spicy, add cayenne. If not, leave it out for a thick, sweet, slightly vinegary barbecue sauce.

Yield: 1 3/4 cups   Serving Size: 1/4 cup

1/2 small yellow or white onion
2 tablespoons water
1 tablespoon olive oil
1 teaspoon minced garlic
1 cup ketchup
1/4 cup packed brown sugar
2 tablespoons apple cider vinegar
1 tablespoon Worcestershire sauce
1 1/2 teaspoons liquid smoke
1 teaspoon oregano
1 teaspoon dry mustard powder
Cayenne to taste (optional)
Salt and pepper to taste
1 3/4 grams kief or finely ground hash

Place onion and water in a food processor or blender and purée. Heat a small saucepan over medium heat and add olive oil. Add onion purée and cook, stirring often, until softened, about 2 to 3 minutes. Add garlic, ketchup, brown sugar, cider vinegar, Worcestershire sauce, liquid smoke, oregano, mustard powder, and cayenne, if using. Mix thoroughly, bring to a simmer, reduce heat to low, cover, and simmer, stirring occasionally, for 10 minutes. Season to taste with salt and pepper. Sprinkle kief or finely ground hash over saucepan and stir to incorporate. Continue to cook and stir until cannabis concentrate is dissolved and evenly mixed into the sauce.

 Liquid smoke is a seasoning made from concentrated hickory or mesquite smoke which imparts a distinctive smoky flavor to foods. You can find it in most grocery stores in the barbecue and steak sauce section.

Sides & Extras

In this chapter you'll find some recipes for what are considered special occasion meal accompaniments and extras including starchy sides, indulgent vegetable dishes, and breads and rolls. I haven't included recipes for simple steamed vegetables in this chapter, because you really don't need a recipe to make such dishes medicated. Simply toss veggies with a medicated vinaigrette-type salad dressing and you'll have a tasty medicated side dish anytime.

It's somewhat of a challenge coming up with a variety of side dish recipes that contain enough butter or oil to give a sufficient cannabis dose without adding extra fats, something most people don't need or desire. If you have access to kief or hash, however, your options broaden. Just make sure there is at least some fat in the recipe to help the THC metabolize.

Cauliflower Gratin

Similar to mac' and cheese, without the mac, this is a rich and creamy indulgent side dish for special occasion dinners.

Yield: 3 cups   Serving Size: 1/2 cup

1/2 small head of cauliflower
1 tablespoon canna-butter
1 1/2 teaspoons Italian seasoning
1/3 cup panko bread crumbs
2 tablespoons unsalted butter
2 tablespoons all-purpose flour
2/3 cup whole milk or half-and-half
1 teaspoon dried parsley
2 green onions, finely chopped
1/4 teaspoon cayenne (optional)
Salt and pepper to taste
1 1/2 grams kief or finely ground dry hash
2/3 cup grated Cheddar cheese

Preheat oven to 350 degrees F. Cut cauliflower into small florets. Blanch in boiling water for 3 minutes. Drain, rinse in cold water to stop the cooking process, and drain again. Set aside. Melt canna-butter over low heat in a small saucepan. Stir in Italian seasoning. Add panko crumbs and stir to coat. Remove from heat and set aside.

Melt butter in a medium saucepan over medium-high heat. Whisk in the flour to make a roux. Continue to whisk constantly and cook until the mixture turns light brown, about 2 minutes. Whisk in the milk or half-and-half until smooth. Stir in parsley, green onions, cayenne, if using, and salt and pepper to taste. Continue to cook, stirring frequently, until mixture has thickened and begins to boil. Remove from heat. Sprinkle in kief or finely ground dry hash until dissolved. Stir in grated cheese until cheese has melted and mixture is smooth. Stir in blanched cauliflower to coat.

Spray 6 small ramekins with cooking spray. Fill 3/4 full with cauliflower mixture. Divide prepared panko crumbs over the tops of the filled ramekins. Bake for about 15 minutes or until bubbly and top has browned.

Freezer Friendly!
Cover extra ramekins of panko-topped cooled gratin with foil and freeze before baking. Place uncovered frozen ramekins in a preheated 375-degree F oven and bake until bubbly and top has browned, about 35 to 40 minutes.

French-Style Roasted Potatoes

The French use nutmeg in savory dishes far more often than Americans do. Here it melds beautifully with lemon zest and olive oil to give these roasted potatoes their tantalizing aroma and amazing flavor.

Yield: 4 cups   Serving Size: 1 cup

1 1/2 pounds russet potatoes
Salt to taste
1 1/2 teaspoons all-purpose flour
1 large yellow onion, diced
1 tablespoon chopped fresh Italian parsley
1/4 teaspoon grated nutmeg
1/2 teaspoon grated lemon zest
Pepper to taste
1/4 cup canna-olive oil
Juice of 1/2 fresh lemon

Preheat oven to 425 degrees F. Peel potatoes and slice into 1/2-inch rounds. Bring a large pot of salted water to a boil. Add potatoes and parboil for 5 minutes. Drain. Butter an 8-inch square baking dish.

In a large mixing bowl, combine flour, onion, parsley, nutmeg, lemon zest, salt, and pepper. Toss to coat. Add the blanched potatoes and canna-olive oil to the bowl and toss to coat well. Place mixture in prepared baking dish. Bake for 20 to 25 minutes or until nicely browned on top. Remove from oven, sprinkle fresh lemon juice over the top and serve immediately.

Freezer Friendly!
Freeze foil-covered unbaked portions in a dish that can go from freezer to oven. Bake at 400 degrees F for about 40 minutes or until cooked and starting to brown. Place under broiler for about 5 minutes and sprinkle with lemon juice before serving.

Real Mashed Potatoes

Creamy potatoes with just the right amount of lumps to let you know they're real and not instant make the quintessential comfort food side dish.

Yield: 4 cups   Serving Size: 1 cup

2 1/2 pounds russet or Yukon Gold potatoes
Salt to taste
3 tablespoons unsalted butter
2 ounces cream cheese, at room temperature
2 grams kief or finely ground hash
Pepper to taste

Bring a large pot of salted water to a boil over high heat. Wash and peel potatoes and cut into 2-inch chunks. Add to water and boil over medium heat until potatoes are soft, about 15 minutes. Drain potatoes in a colander.

Place hot drained potatoes in a large bowl along with butter and cream cheese. Sprinkle kief or finely ground hash over bowl. Use an electric hand mixer to whip potatoes until all ingredients are well combined and little or no lumps remain, according to your preference. Season to taste with salt and pepper.

 Because of the bland, delicate flavor of potatoes, I prefer to make this recipe with kief or hash. You can, however, substitute 3 tablespoons cannabis-infused butter for the unsalted butter and leave out the concentrate.

Steakhouse-Style Creamed Spinach

Fresh spinach enveloped in a creamy sauce makes an indulgent side dish.

Yield: 2 cups   Serving Size: 1/2 cup

1/2 cup heavy cream
1 gram kief or finely ground hash
2 pounds fresh spinach, washed and tough
   stems removed
2 tablespoons unsalted butter

1/2 cup finely chopped shallots
1 1/2 teaspoons minced garlic
3/4 teaspoon salt
1/2 teaspoon black pepper
1/4 teaspoon ground nutmeg

Heat cream in a small saucepan over low heat. Sprinkle kief or hash into cream and stir until dissolved and evenly combined. Set aside.

Wash spinach well. Place a large skillet over medium-high heat. Place wet spinach in skillet and cook, stirring, until spinach is wilted, about 3 minutes. Drain spinach in a strainer or colander, pressing with a large spoon to release as much water as possible. Roughly chop and set aside.

Melt butter in same skillet over medium heat. Add the shallots and garlic and cook, stirring, until softened, about 2 minutes. Add the spinach and cook, stirring, just until the liquid is released. Add the cannabis-infused cream, salt, pepper, and nutmeg. Bring to a simmer, reduce heat to low, and cook until the cream is reduced by half, about 4 to 5 minutes. Serve immediately.

Cheesy Corn Pudding

Sweet corn and sweet red bell peppers blend in a cheesy, eggy, indulgent side dish.

Yield: 3 cups   Serving Size: 1/2 cup

2 tablespoons butter
1 small onion, peeled and diced
1/2 medium red bell pepper, cored,
   seeded and diced
1/2 teaspoon minced garlic

2 cups fresh, frozen, or canned corn kernels
3 grams kief or finely crumbled hash
4 large eggs
1 cup shredded Cheddar or
   Monterey Jack cheese

Preheat oven to 375 degrees F. Butter 6 (6 ounce) ramekins. Heat 2 tablespoons butter in a large skillet over medium heat. Add diced onion and bell pepper and sauté until softened but not yet beginning to brown, about 5 minutes. Add garlic and corn, and sauté for another 3 minutes. Remove from heat and sprinkle in kief or hash and stir until well combined. Set aside.

In a large bowl, whisk the eggs together until frothy and well combined. Stir in cheese with a wooden spoon. Stir in the corn mixture and divide the batter among prepared ramekins. Bake until pudding is set and top is puffed and nicely browned, about 25 minutes.

 Freezer Friendly!
Cover extra individual ramekins of baked corn pudding with foil and freeze. Remove foil and reheat in the microwave, about 4 minutes.

Southern Sweet Potato Casserole

The bright flavor of orange highlights this favorite Southern-style mashed sweet potato casserole. Caramelized marshmallows top it all off. Like many of the recipes in this book, you can bake this casserole in portions that meet your needs. In our photo we baked a double portion in one dish, but you easily use small ramekins to make 8 individual servings, or even choose to bake this as one large casserole.

Yield: 4 cups   Serving Size: 1/2 cup

2 pounds sweet potatoes or yams
1/3 cup canna-butter
1/4 cup packed brown sugar
2 tablespoons frozen orange or
    tangerine juice concentrate, melted
1/4 teaspoon salt
1 teaspoon ground cinnamon
1 teaspoon vanilla extract
1 large egg
1 cup miniature marshmallows
1/3 cup chopped toasted pecans (optional)

Put a large pot of water on to boil. Peel sweet potatoes and cut into small chunks. Boil until tender, about 15 minutes. Drain.

Preheat oven to 350 degrees F. Butter 8 small ramekins (or whatever size baking dish meets your needs).

Use an electric mixer to beat together the boiled sweet potatoes with the canna-butter, brown sugar, melted orange juice concentrate, salt, cinnamon, vanilla, and egg. Continue to beat until smooth. Stir in the pecans, if using. Spoon mixture into the prepared baking dishes. Sprinkle miniature marshmallows around edges of the dish(es), allowing the mashed sweet potatoes to peek through the center. Bake for about 20 minutes or until heated through and tops of marshmallows have browned. Serve hot.

Freezer Friendly!
Freeze extra portions, minus the marshmallows, before baking, covered in foil. Bake frozen casseroles at 375 degrees F for 20 minutes. Add marshmallows and continue to bake until heated, about 20 to 25 more minutes.

Lemon Risotto with Asparagus

Make this amazing risotto when spring asparagus is at its peak. Tart lemon flavor brightens the dish and melds with the Parmesan to create an unforgettable flavor. Find short-grained, starchy arborio rice in Italian markets and well stocked grocery stores.

Yield: 6 cups   Serving Size: 1 1/2 cups

4 cups chicken or vegetable stock
1 tablespoon unsalted butter
1 tablespoon olive oil
2 large shallots, minced
1 teaspoon minced garlic
1 cup arborio rice
1/2 cup dry white wine
1 1/2 cups chopped asparagus pieces, about 1 1/2-inches long
1 large egg
1 gram kief or finely ground dry hash
2 tablespoons lemon juice (juice of 1 small lemon)
1 tablespoon finely grated lemon zest (zest of 1 lemon)
1/2 cup (2 ounces) grated Parmesan cheese
Salt and pepper to taste

Bring stock to a simmer in a small saucepan over medium heat, reduce heat to warm and keep hot.

In a large skillet, heat olive oil over medium-high heat. Sauté the shallots, stirring often, until softened, about 3 minutes. Add garlic and sauté for another minute. Add rice and cook, stirring, until slightly toasted, about 3 minutes. Stir in the wine and cook until it is almost all evaporated. Stir in a cup or so of stock, reduce heat to low, and again, cook until it is almost evaporated before adding more. Continue to cook, adding stock when the previous stock has been almost absorbed, until you have about 1 1/2 cups stock left. Stir in asparagus pieces and 3/4 cup stock and cook until stock is almost absorbed.

While rice is cooking, beat together the egg and kief or hash until the cannabis concentrate is evenly distributed in the egg. Beat in the lemon juice, lemon zest, and Parmesan cheese.

Add the last of the hot stock to the cooking rice and cook for a minute. Remove from heat and stir in the egg mixture until well blended. Return to heat and cook, stirring, until rice is very moist but not quite soup. Season to taste with salt and pepper. Serve immediately.

Freezer Friendly!
Freeze single portions of leftover risotto in microwave-safe containers. To reheat, place frozen risotto in the microwave on High, stopping to stir every minute or so, until heated through, about 4 minutes.

Mushroom Risotto

Creamy rice flavored with earthy mushrooms and sharp Parmesan cheese makes an impressive side dish or even a light entrée. Find short-grained, starchy arborio rice in Italian markets and well stocked grocery stores.

Yield: 7 cups   Serving Size: 1 cup

1 (25-gram) package dried wild mushrooms
5 cups chicken or vegetable stock
1 tablespoon olive oil
1 cup minced celery
2 medium onions, peeled and minced
8 ounces sliced fresh white or cremini mushrooms
1 teaspoon minced garlic
2 cups arborio rice
1/2 cup dry vermouth or dry white wine
3/4 teaspoon dried thyme
2 tablespoons minced fresh Italian parsley, or 1 tablespoon dried parsley
Salt and pepper to taste
3 1/2 grams kief or finely crumbled hash
4 tablespoons unsalted butter
1 1/2 cups (6 ounces) grated Parmesan cheese

Rehydrate dried mushrooms by soaking in hot water for about 10 minutes. Drain and coarsely chop. Heat stock to a simmer; lower heat to keep warm.

Heat olive oil in a large deep skillet over medium-high heat. Add the celery, onions, fresh mushrooms, and rehydrated dried mushrooms and sauté until softened, about 4 minutes. Add garlic and sauté for another minute. Turn up the heat to high, add the rice to the pan, and cook, stirring constantly, for about 4 minutes. The rice will begin to look translucent. Add the vermouth or white wine and keep stirring. Once the vermouth or wine has cooked away, stir in about 1 1/2 cups hot stock along with thyme and parsley. Lower the heat to a simmer. Cook, stirring frequently, until almost all of the stock has been absorbed. Repeat with another ladle of stock. Continue cooking, stirring, and adding stock until it has all been added to the rice and it has been mostly absorbed. Rice should be very moist but not swimming in stock at this point. Season to taste with salt and pepper. Sprinkle in kief or finely crumbled hash and stir until dissolved. Remove from heat and stir in butter and Parmesan until everything is well combined. Let sit for 5 minutes before serving.

Freezer Friendly!
Freeze single portions of leftover risotto in microwave-safe containers. To reheat, place frozen risotto in the microwave on High, stopping to stir every minute or so, until heated through, about 4 minutes.

Macaroni and Cheese for Grown-Ups

Creamy, cheesy, and full of flavor from a variety of strong cheeses, this is not your kid's mac 'n' cheese, even without the cannabis. While you can bake this in one big dish, I like to use small ramekins to make individual servings. Use whatever size baking dishes work best for your needs.

Yield: 5 cups   Serving Size: 1/2 cup

2 teaspoons salt
8 ounces elbow macaroni
1 1/2 grams kief or finely ground dry hash
2 ounces cream cheese
3 tablespoons unsalted butter, divided
2 tablespoons all-purpose flour
2 cups whole milk
1/2 medium onion, peeled and minced
2 teaspoons dry mustard powder

1/2 teaspoon minced garlic
1 bay leaf
1/2 teaspoon paprika
2 ounces grated Parmesan cheese
2 ounces finely crumbled blue cheese
2 1/2 cups shredded extra-sharp Cheddar cheese, divided
Salt and pepper to taste
3/4 cup panko bread crumbs

Add 2 teaspoons salt to a large stockpot of water and bring to a boil over high heat. Add macaroni and cook until flexible but still very *al dente*. Drain.

Preheat oven to 350 degrees F. Butter 10 small ramekins (or whatever size baking dishes meet your portion needs).

Sprinkle kief or hash into cream cheese and whip together to incorporate the cannabis concentrate into the cream cheese.

Melt 2 tablespoons butter in a large saucepan over medium heat. Whisk in flour and cook for 2 minutes, whisking constantly. Gradually whisk in milk. Stir in onion, mustard powder, garlic, bay leaf, and paprika. Increase heat to bring mixture to a boil, then lower heat to a gentle simmer and cook for 10 minutes. Remove from heat and remove bay leaf. Stir in cream cheese/cannabis mixture, grated Parmesan, crumbled blue cheese, and half the shredded Cheddar cheese. Stir until cheese melts. Season to taste with salt and pepper and stir in cooked macaroni.

Divide half the macaroni mixture between the prepared baking dishes. Sprinkle half the remaining cheese on top of macaroni. Top with remaining pasta followed by a sprinkling of the remaining cheese.

In a small skillet over medium heat, melt remaining tablespoon butter. Toss in panko bread crumbs and stir to coat. Sprinkle buttered bread crumbs over the tops of the baking dishes. Bake until heated through and tops have browned, about 20 minutes.

Freezer Friendly!
Freeze cooled, unbaked, foil-covered portions in ramekins. When ready to eat, place frozen ramekin in a preheated 375-degree F oven until filling is bubbly, top is lightly browned, and dish is heated through, about 50 minutes.

Herbed Yeast Dinner Rolls

There's nothing like hot-from-the-oven dinner rolls to turn an ordinary meal into a special occasion. Feel free to leave out the herbs and garlic powder and brush rolls with plain butter after baking, although expect your rolls to have a slightly more pronounced herbal flavor from the cannabis.

Yield: 12 rolls   Serving Size: 2 rolls

1 1/2 teaspoons yeast
2 1/4 teaspoons sugar, divided
1/4 cup very warm water
1/4 cup buttermilk
2 tablespoons whole milk or half-and-half
1 1/2 grams kief or finely ground dry hash
4 teaspoons nonfat dry milk powder
1 1/2 teaspoons salt
1 large egg
2 1/4 cups all-purpose flour
2 tablespoons melted butter
1/2 teaspoon Italian seasoning
1/2 teaspoon garlic powder

Dissolve yeast and 1/4 teaspoon sugar in warm water in a small bowl. Combine buttermilk and milk or half-and-half in a medium bowl. Warm milk mixture in the microwave for about 20 seconds. Stir kief or finely ground dry hash into the warm milk to combine and dissolve.

In the large bowl of an electric mixer fitted with the dough hook, combine buttermilk mixture, remaining 2 teaspoons sugar, dry milk powder, salt, and egg and mix well. Stir in the yeast mixture until combined. Add the flour in two additions and let the machine knead the dough for about 5 minutes. Shape dough into a ball and place in a buttered bowl, turning to coat the surface. Cover bowl with a clean kitchen towel and place in a draft-free spot to allow the dough to rise until doubled in size, about 1 1/2 hours.

Grease a large baking sheet (or cover with parchment paper). Punch the dough down and divide into 12 equal pieces. Roll each piece into a small ball. Arrange balls on the prepared baking sheet. Cover with clean kitchen towel and let rise in a draft-free place for 45 minutes.

Preheat oven to 350 degrees F. Bake rolls for about 30 minutes or until golden brown. While rolls bake, melt butter and mix with Italian seasoning and garlic powder. Brush rolls with herbed butter as soon as they come out of the oven. Serve hot.

 Freezer Friendly!
Freeze unbaked rolls in a single layer. Remove to a plastic freezer bag when frozen. When ready to eat, bring the number of rolls you need to room temperature, which will take about 2 hours. Bake as directed above.

Buttermilk Biscuits

Fluffy buttermilk biscuits hot out of the oven can make any meal special.

Yield: 8 biscuits   Serving Size: 1 biscuit

2 cups flour
1 tablespoon baking powder
1/2 teaspoon baking soda
1 teaspoon sugar
1/4 cup cold canna-butter
2 tablespoons vegetable shortening
2/3 cup buttermilk
1 tablespoon unsalted butter, melted

     Preheat oven to 425 degrees F. Place flour, baking powder, baking soda, and sugar in the bowl of a food processor and pulse a few times to mix. Add cannabis-infused butter and shortening and pulse a few times until you have a mixture that resembles coarse crumbs. Spoon into a medium bowl. (Alternately use 2 knives to cut the fat into the dry ingredients.) Add buttermilk and stir just until dough holds together. Mix and knead the dough as little as possible in order to keep the biscuits tender.
     On a lightly floured surface, roll dough into a disc about an inch high and 6-inches in diameter. Use a round cookie cutter or a glass about 2 1/2 inches in diameter to cut out 8 biscuits, rerolling dough as necessary. Arrange on a baking sheet that's been covered with parchment paper. Brush top of biscuits with melted butter and bake until golden brown, about 15 minutes. Cool on a wire rack for 3 minutes before serving.

 Freezer Friendly!
Freeze unbaked biscuits in a single layer before removing to a freezer bag. Bake on a parchment-lined baking sheet at 400 degrees F for 5 minutes, brush with melted butter, and bake until golden brown, about 15 minutes.

Corn Bread

Corn bread, hot and sweet from the oven, can turn even the most humble meal into an event!

Yield: 9 pieces   Serving Size: 1 piece

1 cup cornmeal
1 cup all-purpose flour
1/2 cup sugar
3/4 teaspoon baking soda

1/2 teaspoon salt
2 large eggs
1 cup buttermilk
1/2 cup canna-butter, melted

Preheat oven to 375 degrees F. Grease an 8-inch square baking pan with butter or vegetable shortening. In a large bowl, combine cornmeal, flour, sugar, baking soda, and salt. Stir to combine.

In a separate bowl, whisk together eggs, buttermilk, and slightly cooled melted cannabis-infused butter. Stir wet ingredients into dry ingredients just until combined. Pour batter into pan and smooth out surface with a spatula. Bake until a toothpick inserted in the center comes out clean and bread is starting to brown on the edges, about 25 to 30 minutes. Cool in pan for 5 minutes before cutting into 8 pieces and serving warm. Store leftovers in a tightly sealed plastic bag for up to 3 days.

Garlic Bread Deluxe

This recipe crosses garlic bread with a grilled cheese sandwich to make the perfect anytime snack or a great side dish for an Italian-style pasta dinner.

Yield: 2 half-loaves   Serving Size: 1/4 of one loaf half

2 tablespoons unsalted canna-butter
2 tablespoons canna-olive oil
2 teaspoon minced garlic
1/4 cup grated Parmesan cheese

1/2 cup shredded whole or part-skim
  mozzarella cheese
1 (1-pound) loaf French or Italian bread
2 teaspoons Italian seasoning

Preheat oven to 375 degrees F. In a small saucepan, or in the microwave, heat cannabis-infused butter and olive oil together with garlic until just melted. In a separate bowl, mix together Parmesan and mozzarella cheeses.

Cut the loaf of bread lengthwise down the center. Use a pastry brush to apply the butter mixture liberally to both cut surfaces. Sprinkle with Italian seasoning and cheese mixture, dividing ingredients between the 2 loaf halves. Bake for about 12 to 15 minutes or until cheese is melted and starting to brown and bread is toasted.

 Freezer Friendly!
Tightly wrap unbaked loaf half in aluminum foil and freeze. Unwrap and bake frozen garlic cheese bread at 375 degrees F for about 18 to 20 minutes or until heated through and cheese is melted and starting to brown.

Beverages

Beverages are one of the easiest way to ingest edible cannabis, although with nearly all drinks you will need access to kief, hash, or tinctures. I went over my thoughts on tinctures in Chapter 1 (page 22) and accordingly have not included recipes using them here. However, if you like using tinctures in food, simply add your normal dose to your favorite drink, stir, and you are good to go.

It's just as easy to add hash or kief to hot drinks. Try adding 1/4 gram or so into your morning tea or coffee (add whole milk, half-and-half, or cream to help it metabolize). Stir to combine and help dissolve the concentrate and enjoy.

Mango Lassi

India's version of a smoothie is tangy with yogurt and slightly spiced with exotic cardamom (well, not THAT exotic—find it in the supermarket).

Yield: 2 cups   Serving Size: 1 cup

1 cup frozen mango pieces
   (or 1 large ripe mango, chopped and frozen)
1 cup plain whole milk yogurt
1/2 cup whole milk or buttermilk
1/2 gram kief or finely ground dry hash
1/2 teaspoon ground cardamom

    Place frozen mango, yogurt, milk or buttermilk, kief or ground dry hash, and cardamom in blender or food processor. Purée until smooth. If drink is too thick, add additional milk or buttermilk as needed.

Devilishly Good Orange Smoothie

When I first visited California as a young child, I remember Orange Julius stands, with their signature red devil logo, dotting the landscape. This sweet citrus drink now seems relegated to mall food courts, if you can find it at all. This cannabis-infused version tastes close to the original.

Yield: 1 cup   Serving Size: 1 cup

3 tablespoons frozen orange juice concentrate, thawed
1/2 cup whole milk or half-and-half
1/4 gram kief or finely ground dry hash
1 tablespoon sugar
1/4 teaspoon vanilla extract
2 or 3 ice cubes

    Place orange juice concentrate, milk or half-and-half, kief or ground hash, sugar, and vanilla in a blender and purée until smooth and frothy. Add ice cubes and purée until frosty and ice is incorporated into the drink. Serve immediately.

Peaches and Cream Smoothie

This thick, creamy smoothie is almost like peachy ice cream, with a lot less fat.

Yield: 2 cups   Serving Size: 1 cup

3/4 cup whole milk or half-and-half
1/2 gram kief or finely ground dry hash
1 1/2 cups sliced peaches, frozen
2 tablespoons frozen orange juice concentrate
1 tablespoon honey
1/2 cup vanilla frozen yogurt
1/8 teaspoon nutmeg
2 peach slices for garnish (optional)

   Place milk or half-and-half, kief or ground dry hash, frozen peaches, orange juice concentrate, honey, and frozen yogurt in a blender and blend until smooth. Divide between 2 glasses and sprinkle with nutmeg. Garnish with an additional peach slice, if desired.

Piña Colada Smoothie

Sweet pineapple, banana, and coconut meld perfectly in this tropical smoothie that is sweet enough to stand in for dessert. By freezing the fruit first, there's no need to use flavor-diluting ice to get a frosty smoothie.

Yield: 2 cups   Serving Size: 1 cup

1/4 cup cream of coconut
1/2 gram kief or finely ground hash
1 small banana, peeled, cut into chunks, and frozen
1 1/2 cups pineapple cubes, frozen
1 1/2 cups pineapple juice
2 small pineapple slices and 2 maraschino cherries for garnish (optional)

   Stir the cream of coconut in the can to blend, as it often separates. Measure out 1/4 cup and place in blender or food processor with kief or finely ground hash, frozen banana, pineapple, and pineapple juice. Process until smooth. Divide between two glasses. Garnish with pineapple slice and cherry, if desired.

 Coconut cream or **cream of coconut** is a sweet, syrupy coconut-flavored mixture primarily used for making piña coladas. Coco Lopez is the most commonly found brand. Do not confuse cream of coconut with unsweetened coconut milk or cream.

Strawberry Licuado

Make this refreshing drink, the Latin American version of a smoothie, when fresh strawberries are at their peak season for best flavor. Substitute frozen berries at other times of year.

Yield: 3 cups   Serving Size: 1 1/2 cups

1 cup whole milk
1/2 gram kief or finely ground dry hash
1 pint fresh ripe strawberries, stemmed
1 tablespoon sugar or honey, more to taste
4 or 5 ice cubes
2 whole strawberries for garnish (optional)

Whirl all ingredients except garnish together in a blender until smooth and ice is crushed. Garnish glass with whole strawberry, if desired. Serve immediately.

New York-Style Chocolate Egg Cream

Non-native New Yorkers are always surprised to learn that egg creams contain no eggs. Use Fox's U-Bet brand chocolate syrup, if you can find it, for the most authentic version. Otherwise, use whatever brand you have on hand.

Yield: 1 1/2 cups   Serving Size: 1 1/2 cups

1/2 cup whole milk or half-and-half
1/4 gram kief or hash
2 tablespoons chocolate syrup
1 cup bottled seltzer water

Heat milk or half-and-half in a small pan over medium heat (or heat until very hot but not boiling in the microwave). Stir in hash or kief until dissolved. Chill until cold.

Pour chilled milk mixture into a tall glass. Stir in chocolate syrup until combined. Slowly pour in seltzer water. Serve immediately.

Variation: Turn this soda fountain staple into an ice cream soda by floating a scoop of vanilla or chocolate ice cream in the drink.

Iced Café Latte

If the weather is too hot for regular coffee, try it over ice instead.

Yield: 1 1/2 cups   Serving Size: 1 1/2 cups

Sugar to taste
3/4 cup strongly brewed coffee or espresso
3/4 cup whole milk or half-and-half
1/4 gram kief or hash

Add sugar to taste to black coffee; stir to dissolve. Chill sweetened coffee in the refrigerator until cold. In a small saucepan over medium-low heat, warm milk or half-and-half—do not boil. Add kief or hash to milk and stir to dissolve. Remove from heat and cool slightly. Add milk mixture to chilled coffee, stir, and pour into a tall glass filled with ice. Serve immediately.

Hot Café Mocha

Chocolaty Hot Café Mocha is so easy to make, you'll never go to a coffee house again.

Yield: 1 1/2 cups   Serving Size: 1 1/2 cups

3/4 cup whole milk
1/4 gram kief or hash
2 tablespoons chocolate syrup
3/4 cup strongly brewed coffee or espresso
Whipped cream and additional chocolate syrup for garnish (optional)

Heat milk in a small saucepan over low heat—do not boil. Add kief or hash to milk and stir until dissolved. Add milk mixture and chocolate syrup to a large coffee mug and stir until well combined. Add hot coffee; stir to combine. Garnish with whipped cream and additional chocolate syrup, if desired. For a decorative look, do not add syrup to coffee. Instead swirl or stripe it inside a glass mug before adding the combined coffee/milk mixture.
Variation: Chill Hot Café Mocha until cold. Serve over ice for Iced Café Mocha.

Triple-Chocolate Hot Chocolate

Three different types of chocolate contribute to the rich favor of this classic hot beverage.

Yield: 1 1/4 cups   Serving Size: 1 1/4 cup

3/4 cup whole milk
1/4 cup heavy cream
1/4 gram kief or hash
2 ounces bittersweet or semisweet chocolate, chopped
2 ounces milk chocolate, chopped
2 teaspoons cocoa powder
1/8 teaspoon salt
Miniature marshmallows or whipped cream
    for garnish (optional)

  In a small saucepan over medium low heat, combine milk and cream. Heat, but do not boil. Stir in kief or hash and heat, stirring, until dissolved. Stir in chocolate and cocoa and heat, stirring constantly, until chocolate is melted and mixture is hot. If cocoa lumps form, whisk mixture to remove them before pouring into a serving mug. Garnish with marshmallows or whipped cream, if desired.

Masala Chai Tea

There is no end to the variations on Masala Chai Tea. The spice blend below is a good starting point, but feel free to experiment with other quantities and spices to find your own perfect mix.

Yield: 3 cups   Serving Size: 1 1/2 cups

1 whole cardamom pod
2 whole cloves
1/2 cinnamon stick
1/8 teaspoon ground black pepper
1/4 teaspoon ground ginger
2 cups water
1 cup whole milk
2 tablespoons sugar, more to taste
1 tablespoon loose black tea
1/2 gram kief or ground hash

Lightly crush cardamom pod and place in a small saucepan along with cloves, cinnamon stick, pepper, and ginger. Add water and bring to a boil over medium heat. Remove from heat, cover, and let steep for 5 minutes. Add milk and sugar to the pan and return to medium heat. Bring to a boil. Remove from heat and stir in tea. Cover and let steep for 3 to 4 minutes. Strain through a fine mesh strainer. Stir in kief or finely ground hash until dissolved. Pour into mugs and serve immediately.

Variation: For a refreshing change, make as above and cool. Serve over ice for Iced Chai Tea.

Thai-Style Iced Tea

Not only is Thai iced tea a refreshing drink, it makes the perfect sweet counterpoint to hot and spicy foods. Thai tea consists of black tea sometimes flavored with vanilla and other spices and often with a little yellow food coloring added (don't ask me why). Wangderm is a popular brand commonly found at US world market stores and tea shops. If you can't find Thai Tea, brew a cup of strong black tea and add 1/8 teaspoon vanilla extract to this recipe.

Yield: 1 1/4 cups/1 serving   Serving Size: 1 1/4 cups

1 cup strongly brewed Thai tea
1/4 gram kief or hash
6 to 8 ice cubes
1/4 cup canned sweetened condensed milk

While the tea is still hot, stir in the kief or hash until dissolved. Set aside to cool or refrigerate. When ready to use, fill a large glass with ice. Pour in the tea/cannabis mixture and the sweetened condensed milk. Stir to blend and enjoy.

Thai-Style Iced Coffee

Thai iced coffee is a wonderful hot-weather drink and a handy way to use up extra coffee. Brew extra morning coffee and make it a little stronger than usual to balance out the sweetness of the milk.

Yield: 1 1/4 cups/1 serving   Serving Size: 1 1/4 cups

1 cup strongly brewed coffee
1/4 gram kief or hash
6 to 8 ice cubes
1/4 cup canned sweetened condensed milk

While the coffee is still hot, stir in the kief or hash until dissolved. Set aside to cool or refrigerate. When ready to use, fill a large glass with ice. Pour in the coffee/cannabis mixture and the sweetened condensed milk. Stir to blend and enjoy.

Variations: Traditional Thai Iced Coffee and Thai Iced Tea are very sweet. If, like me, you prefer a less cloying version, use 2 tablespoons sweetened condensed milk mixed with 2 tablespoons evaporated milk.

Desserts

Sweet treats are the most popular way of ingesting marijuana edibles, so much so that some people seem to think that's all you can make with cannabis. I attribute the popularity of desserts largely to the fact that it's easy and discreet to munch on a cookie or brownie anywhere without arising suspicion. Also, these foods are easy to portion control . . . providing you have the willpower to not go back for seconds.

Portion control gets a little trickier when it comes to dividing cakes and pies. The nearby availability of tempting cakes and pies is too much for some people to resist, which can result in not only too many calories, but too much medication. That's why, whenever possible, I've divided the recipes into smaller portions such as cupcakes instead of cakes and tarts instead of whole pies. Of course, you'll also find freezing instructions whenever possible so you can keep extra portions out of easy reach.

It's relatively easy to incorporate cannabis into many dessert recipes as they often contain significant amounts of butter, which you can substitute for canna-butter. Check through your favorite recipes and see which ones you can adapt for cannabis cooking.

Lemon Berry Swirl Cheesecake Tarts

Creamy cheesecake gets a flavor boost from tart lemons and sweet berries. While the pound of frozen berries called for in this recipe will make about 1 3/4 cups strained fruit coulis, far more than you need, you can freeze leftovers of this versatile ingredient in a lidded freezer container or in ice cube trays (so you can easily defrost small amounts later). Bring to room temperature and use as a sauce for ice cream or fruit, as a syrup on pancakes, as an all-natural drink or yogurt flavoring, or to decorate dessert plates with a splash of edible color.

Yield: 8 (4¹/₂-inch) cheesecake tarts, or 1 (6- to 8-inch) cake   Serving Size: 1 tart/¹/₈ recipe

Berry Coulis
1 pound bag frozen mixed berries
1/2 cup water
1/3 cup sugar

Crust
2 cups crushed graham cracker crumbs
1/2 cup melted canna-butter

Filling
2 pounds cream cheese
1 cup sugar
1 teaspoon vanilla extract
1/4 cup lemon juice
1 tablespoon lemon zest
3 large eggs
2 cups sour cream

In a medium saucepan, combine berries, water, and sugar and bring to a boil over medium heat. Cook for 5 minutes. Remove from heat. Use a blender, immersion blender, or food processor to purée mixture. Strain through a fine sieve to remove seeds and solids. Set aside.

Preheat oven to 350 degrees F. Mix together graham cracker crumbs and melted canna-butter until well blended. Place a generous 1/4 cup crumb mixture in each of 8 (4 1/2-inch) tart pans, preferably with removable bottoms, or a 6- to 8-inch springform pan. Press crumbs over bottom and up the sides of pan(s). Bake crust(s) until set, about 6 minutes. Set aside. Reduce oven temperature to 300 degrees F. Place a large casserole dish of very hot water in the oven.

In a large bowl beat cream cheese and 1 cup sugar with an electric mixer on high speed until smooth and fluffy. Beat in the vanilla extract, lemon juice, and lemon zest, one at a time, until well mixed. Beat in eggs one at a time, taking care the previous egg is incorporated before adding the next. Reduce mixer speed to low and beat in sour cream just until well blended.

Fill each tart crust about halfway with filling, or alternately pour into prepared crust in springform pan. Drop several dollops of fruit coulis onto filling (about 1 1/2 to 2 teaspoons in each tart, or 4 to 5 tablespoons onto a larger cake). Top with remaining filling. Take a blunt knife and, taking care not to disturb the crust on the bottom and side, gently move it though the filling to create swirls of berry coulis in the cheesecake. Place filled tarts or cake on a baking sheet and place in oven. Bake for 40 minutes (1 hour if making a single cake in a springform pan). Turn off oven but do not open the door for 1 hour.

Transfer to a wire rack to cool completely before wrapping and chilling in the refrigerator for at least 4 hours before removing from tart pans or springform pan and serving.

Freezer Friendly!
Wrap extra cheesecake portions in plastic wrap and freeze. Thaw in the refrigerator and enjoy.

Key Lime in the Coconut Crust Tartlets

Here's my culinary ode to the late great Harry Nilsson. Lime and coconut are two great tastes that go great together, and there's no better example than these tartlets. If you can't find tiny Key limes to juice, you can substitute regular lime juice and still get great results. Surprise! True Key lime pies are not green. Whenever you see one that is, you'll know that food coloring was at play.

Yield: 4 (4½-inch) tarts   Serving Size: 1 tart

Crust
¾ cup graham cracker crumbs
½ cup sweetened flaked coconut
¼ cup melted canna-butter

Filling
¾ cup sweetened condensed milk
⅓ cup Key lime juice
2 large eggs

Topping
1 cup sour cream
3 tablespoons confectioners' sugar

Preheat oven to 375 degrees F. Mix crushed graham crackers and coconut with melted butter until evenly combined. Divide between 4 (4 ½-inch diameter) tart pans, preferably with removable bottoms. Use your fingers to press the mixture into an even layer over the bottom and up the side of each pan. Place pans on a baking sheet and bake until crust is set and lightly browned, about 10 to 12 minutes. Remove from oven and set aside. Reduce oven temperature to 325 degrees F.

In a large bowl, whisk together sweetened condensed milk, lime juice, and eggs until smooth. Divide the filling mixture among the 4 prepared tart crusts. Bake for 15 minutes. Remove from oven and cool on a wire rack for 15 minutes before chilling in the refrigerator for at least 2 hours.

Whisk together sour cream and confectioners' sugar. Spread a thick layer of sour cream over the chilled tarts. Keep chilled until ready to serve. Store leftover tarts, covered, in the refrigerator for up to 3 days.

Chocolate Peanut Butter Tarts

These tarts are rich, creamy, and a peanut butter lover's dream. Making this recipe in smaller tart pans makes it easier to keep from overindulging, but you can also make it as 1 large 9-inch pie that can be cut into 12 small individual servings after chilling.

Yield: 6 (5-inch) tarts   Serving Size: 1/2 tart

Crust
1 1/4 cups chocolate crumbs (made from slightly more than 1/2 of a 9-ounce box of Nestle's Famous Chocolate Wafer cookies)
4 tablespoons butter, melted

Filling
8 ounces cream cheese
1 cup creamy peanut butter
2 1/2 grams kief or finely ground dry hash

3/4 cup heavy cream
3/4 cup packed brown sugar
2 teaspoons vanilla extract

Topping
2/3 cup heavy cream
2 tablespoons corn syrup, preferably dark
4 ounces bittersweet or semisweet chocolate
1/2 cup chopped roasted salted peanuts

Preheat oven to 375 degrees F. Stir the chocolate cookie crumbs and melted butter together with a fork until combined. Place about 1/3 cup crumb mixture in each of 6 (5-inch) tart shells with removable bottoms. Press crumbs against the sides and bottoms of tart pans in an even layer. Bake for 10 minutes. Remove from oven and cool completely before filling.

Place cream cheese and peanut butter in a large bowl and beat with an electric mixer on high speed until light and fluffy. Sprinkle kief or finely ground dry hash over mixture and beat until well incorporated. Transfer to another bowl if using a stand mixer, and place 3/4 cup heavy cream in mixer bowl (no need to wash bowl in between). If using a hand mixer, place cream in a medium bowl.

Beat cream on medium speed until frothy and slightly thickened. Beat in brown sugar and vanilla. Increase speed to high and beat until cream forms soft peaks. Stir 1/3 whipped cream into peanut butter mixture to lighten it. Fold in remaining whipped cream just until incorporated into peanut butter mixture. Divide among the tart crusts. Place a piece of plastic wrap directly onto the filling and chill in the refrigerator for at least 2 hours before adding topping.

Add 2/3 cup heavy cream, corn syrup, and chocolate to a small saucepan over low heat. Heat, stirring, until chocolate has melted. Stir rapidly until mixture is smooth. Pour chocolate mixture over the chilled tarts. Sprinkle chopped peanuts on top and refrigerate for at least 1 hour before serving.

Freezer Friendly!
Wrap extra tarts (or portions of tarts) in plastic wrap and freeze. When ready to eat, thaw in the refrigerator and enjoy. These tarts are even delicious frozen, so no actual need to thaw if you're in a hurry.

Summer Fruit Cobbler

Use a mix of the freshest fruits you can find at the market for this old-fashioned fruit dessert—peaches and other stone fruits along with all sorts of berries work well. In fact, this recipe works with most any type of fresh or frozen fruit, so it's adaptable year-round. No matter what, the delicate biscuit crust ties it perfectly together. Canna-butter can lend a green hue to the biscuit topping. Avoid this by using regular butter in the topping and adding 2 1/2 grams kief or hash to the filling instead.

Yield: 1 (8-inch) square pan   Serving Size: 1/9 of pan

1/2 cup plus 1 tablespoon sugar, divided
4 teaspoons cornstarch
4 cups summer fruit, such as berries and
    peeled, sliced stone fruits
2 tablespoons lemon juice
2 tablespoons cold water
1/8 teaspoon ground cardamom (optional)

1 1/2 cups all-purpose flour
1 1/2 teaspoons baking powder
1/2 teaspoon baking soda
1/4 teaspoon salt
1/3 cup canna-butter
3/4 cup plus 1 tablespoon heavy cream

Preheat oven to 400 degrees F. Grease an 8×8-inch glass or ceramic baking dish with butter or shortening.

In a large saucepan stir together 1/4 cup sugar and cornstarch. Add fruit, lemon juice, water, and cardamom, if using, and stir to combine. Bring to a boil over medium-high heat, stirring constantly. Reduce heat and simmer for 5 minutes, stirring frequently. Remove from heat and pour into prepared baking dish.

In the bowl of a food processor combine flour, 1/4 cup sugar, baking powder, baking soda, and salt and pulse to combine. Add cannabis-infused butter and pulse until butter is well combined and mixture resembles coarse crumbs. Alternately use a pastry blender or 2 knives to cut the butter into the dry ingredients. Add 3/4 cup cream and pulse (or stir with wooden spoon if not using food processor) until just combined and a soft dough forms.

Turn dough out onto a lightly floured surface and knead a few times. Roll out to about 1/2-inch thickness. Use a 3-inch cookie cutter (or the top of a drinking glass approximately that size) to cut the dough into 9 biscuits (gather scraps and reroll as necessary).

Brush biscuits with remaining tablespoon cream and sprinkle top with remaining tablespoon sugar. Place biscuits on top of fruit filling, touching but not crowded (3 rows of 3). Bake for about 25 minutes or until tops of biscuits are lightly browned. Serve warm. Top with ice cream, if desired.

Freezer Friendly!
Cool completely and freeze in a lidded container. Reheat frozen cobbler in a 375-degree F oven for about 40 minutes or until fruit is bubbling.

French Vanilla Ice Cream

Rich vanilla ice cream makes a perfect blank canvas for all kinds of desserts. Think sundaes, milk shakes, ice cream sodas, and more.

Yield: 4 cups   Serving Size: 1/2 cup

1 vanilla bean
1 1/2 cups heavy cream
1 1/2 cups whole milk
2 grams kief or hash

1/2 cup sugar, divided
4 large egg yolks
1 1/2 teaspoons real vanilla extract
1/8 teaspoon salt

Split vanilla bean lengthwise and scrape out the interior pulp and seeds. Place pod, seeds, and pulp in a saucepan with cream, milk, kief or hash, and 1/4 cup sugar. Cook over medium-low heat, stirring frequently, until hot but not boiling and kief or hash has dissolved.

In a medium bowl, whisk together egg yolks, remaining 1/4 cup sugar, vanilla extract, and salt. Whisking quickly to avoid scrambling the eggs, add about 1 1/2 cups hot milk mixture into eggs. Whisk egg mixture back into pan of milk mixture and cook over low heat, stirring constantly, until heated through and slightly thickened—do not boil! Remove vanilla bean. Transfer mixture to a bowl and allow to cool to room temperature. Cover and refrigerate until completely chilled, at least 3 hours. Transfer to an ice cream maker and process according to manufacturer's instructions.

Hot Fudge Dessert Sauce

Rich and chocolaty, this sauce can dress up all kinds of desserts like ice cream, pound cake, or fresh fruits. It freezes well, so you can store and have it ready for use at a moment's notice.

Yield: 2 cups   Serving Size: 1/4 cup

3 (1-ounce) squares unsweetened chocolate
1/4 cup canna-butter
1/4 teaspoon salt

1 2/3 cups sugar
1/2 (12-ounce) can evaporated milk
1 teaspoon vanilla extract

In the top of a double boiler (or a metal bowl placed over a saucepan of simmering water), melt chocolate and cannabis-infused butter. Add the salt and stir to combine. Stir in sugar in 3 additions, stirring to incorporate before adding more. Slowly stir in 1/2 can of evaporated milk, a little at a time, until everything is completely mixed. Continue to cook and stir until sugar is completely melted and sauce is smooth, about 3 minutes. Stir in vanilla extract. Use now for hot fudge sauce or cool completely, package in a lidded container, and refrigerate. Microwave for about 10 seconds to reheat before using.

Freezer Friendly!
Freeze Hot Fudge Dessert Sauce and Butterscotch Dessert Sauce (page 139) in lidded freezer containers. Spoon out amount needed and microwave for 10 to 20 seconds. Watch closely, these dessert sauces can boil over in a matter of seconds.

Butterscotch Dessert Sauce

Use this buttery sweet sauce on ice cream, cakes, or even fresh fruit.

Yield: 1 1/4 cups/10 servings   Serving Size: 2 tablespoons

1 cup packed dark brown sugar
1/2 cup heavy cream
1/3 cup light corn syrup
2 tablespoons butter

1 teaspoon distilled white vinegar
1/2 teaspoon salt
2 1/2 grams kief or hash
1 1/2 teaspoons vanilla extract

In a medium saucepan over high heat, combine brown sugar, cream, corn syrup, butter, vinegar, and salt. Bring to a boil, stirring occasionally. Reduce heat to low and simmer for 3 minutes. Stir in hash or kief and cook, stirring, until dissolved. Remove from heat and stir in vanilla. Serve hot or chilled.

Dark Chocolate Truffles

These truffle candies are rich, dense, decadent mouthfuls of joy with a creamy chocolate center coated in cocoa powder.

Yield: 30 (1-inch) truffles   Serving Size: 2 truffles

1/2 pound good quality bittersweet (not
    unsweetened) chocolate, chopped
3/4 cup heavy whipping cream

3 1/2 grams kief or finely ground hash
About 3/4 cup cocoa powder

Place 1/2 pound of the chopped chocolate in a medium mixing bowl. Heat cream in a small saucepan over medium heat. When hot but not boiling, sprinkle in hash or kief and continue to cook, stirring, until cannabis is dissolved and evenly incorporated in the cream. Bring to a boil and immediately remove from heat and pour over the chopped chocolate in the mixing bowl. Let stand for 1 minute then stir until thoroughly blended and mixture is smooth. Cover and let cool to room temperature before placing in the refrigerator to chill for at least 2 hours before proceeding.

Line a baking sheet with parchment paper. Use a small scoop or melon baller to scoop out small 1-inch balls of filling and place on the baking sheet. Lightly coat your hands with cocoa powder and form each portion into a round ball. Roll each ball in cocoa powder until coated. Chill. Bring to room temperature before serving.

Freezer Friendly!
Freeze truffles in a single layer on the lined baking sheet. Bring to room temperature and enjoy.

Molten Chocolate Lava Cakes

As soon as you cut into one of these little chocolate cakes, hot chocolate lava starts flowing out for a to-die-for decadent chocolate meal finale. Made according to recipe, these cakes will be strongly dosed (assuming you used decent quality material to make your butter). Lightweights will want to swap 2 to 3 tablespoons regular unsalted butter for an equal amount of canna-butter.

Yield: 6 cakes Serving Size: 1 cake

8 ounces chopped bittersweet chocolate
6 tablespoons canna-butter
6 tablespoons unsalted butter
3 large eggs
3 large egg yolks
1/3 cup plus about 2 tablespoons sugar
6 tablespoons all-purpose flour
Whipped cream for serving (optional)

Preheat oven to 350 degrees F. Butter 6 (6-ounce) ramekins and lightly dust with flour. Set aside on a baking sheet.

Place 6 ounces of the chopped chocolate, along with the butter and canna-butter, in the top of a double boiler (or a metal bowl suspended over barely simmering water). Melt, stirring frequently, until smooth. Set aside to cool slightly.

Use an electric mixer at medium high speed to beat together the eggs, egg yolks, and sugar until thick and pale yellow in color, about 5 minutes. Reduce speed to low and mix in flour, followed by the chocolate mixture. Increase speed to medium and beat until mixture is smooth and glossy, about another minute.

Divide half the batter between the 6 prepared ramekins. Sprinkle remaining chopped chocolate over batter and cover with remaining batter. Bake until just set—center will still be jiggly—about 10 minutes. All ovens vary, so watch carefully and do not overbake this recipe or the cakes will lose their lava component (although they will still be tasty). This recipe isn't difficult, but there is a very short "perfect" window in which to remove the cakes from the oven. A minute more and they're overcooked, a minute too little and the batter will be a runny mess.

Freezer Friendly!
Cover and freeze unbaked ramekins. When ready to eat, place frozen ramekin in a preheated 400-degree F oven for about 13 to 15 minutes or until just set with a not quite cooked center.

Carrot Cake Cupcakes with Cream Cheese Icing

Classic moist, spiced carrot cake is crowned with sweet and tangy cream cheese icing for an unforgettable cupcake. If you consider yourself a cannabis lightweight, make this recipe using just the cannabis-infused oil for a light dose. Otherwise, use the canna-oil along with kief or hash for a stronger dose.

Yield: 18 cupcakes　　Serving Size: 1 cupcake

Cupcakes
1/2 cup neutral canna-oil
1 1/2 grams kief or finely crumbled hash
   (optional) (see note above)
1 cup plus 2 tablespoons all-purpose flour
3/4 cup sugar
1/4 cup firmly packed brown sugar
1/2 teaspoon baking powder
1/2 teaspoon baking soda
1/4 teaspoon salt
1 teaspoon cinnamon
1/2 teaspoon dried ginger
1/4 teaspoon ground nutmeg

1/8 teaspoon ground cloves
2 large eggs
1 teaspoon vanilla
1/2 cup crushed or puréed pineapple,
   fresh or canned
1 1/3 cups grated carrots

Icing
8 ounces cream cheese
1/2 cup unsalted butter, softened
3 1/2 cups confectioners' sugar
1 teaspoon vanilla extract

Preheat oven to 350 degrees F. Line 18 muffin pans with paper cupcake liners. If you plan on augmenting this recipe with kief or hash (see note above), heat canna-oil in a small pan over low heat; do not boil. Stir in kief or hash until dissolved. Set aside.

In the large bowl of an electric mixer, mix together flour, sugar, brown sugar, baking powder, baking soda, salt, cinnamon, ginger, nutmeg, and cloves.

Mix oil into the dry ingredients then beat in eggs, one at a time, followed by vanilla. Stir in pineapple and carrots and mix until blended. Divide batter among prepared muffin cups, filling each slightly more than half-full. Bake for about 20 minutes or until a toothpick inserted into the center of a cake comes out clean. Cool in pan for about 10 minutes before removing cupcakes to a wire rack to cool completely before frosting.

To prepare icing, use an electric mixer to beat together cream cheese with softened butter for about 3 minutes or until light and fluffy. Gradually beat in confectioners' sugar, then vanilla extract. Frost cooled cupcakes with cream cheese icing. Store frosted cupcakes in the refrigerator. Bring to room temperature 30 minutes before serving.

 Freezer Friendly!
Freeze frosted cupcakes in freezer bags, stacked between layers of waxed paper. Thaw at room temperature or in the refrigerator. Freeze extra icing in lidded containers until the next time you bake.

Mini Pineapple Upside-Down Cakes

Caramel-infused pineapple covers moist, delicate cake for an unforgettable meal finale that looks as great as it tastes. For portion control, I've baked these in 8 individual ramekins that conveniently happen to be the exact size of a single slice of pineapple. You could also bake this as one large cake in a 9-inch cast-iron skillet or 9-inch baking pan.

Yield: 8 mini cakes   Serving Size: 1 cake

1/3 cup unsalted butter, at room temperature
2/3 cup packed brown sugar
8 canned pineapple slices, drained,
    juice reserved (about 1/4 cup)
8 maraschino cherries
1 1/2 cups all-purpose flour
2 teaspoons baking powder
1 teaspoon cinnamon
3/4 teaspoon salt

5 tablespoons canna-butter,
    at room temperature
3 tablespoons unsalted butter,
    at room temperature
1/2 cup sugar
1/2 cup buttermilk
1 1/2 teaspoons vanilla extract
2 eggs yolks
2 egg whites

Preheat oven to 350 degrees F. Butter 8 (6 ounce/3 1/2-inch diameter) ramekins. With an electric mixer, cream together 1/3 cup butter and brown sugar until evenly combined. Divide between the ramekins and spread evenly over the bottoms. Place in oven until sugar melts, about 10 minutes. Remove pan from oven and place a single pineapple slice in each ramekin. Place a maraschino cherry in the center of each pineapple slice. Set aside but keep oven on.

In a small bowl, stir together flour, baking powder, cinnamon, and salt. In a large bowl beat together the canna-butter, 3 tablespoons unsalted butter, and 1/2 cup sugar until light and fluffy. Beat in the reserved pineapple juice, buttermilk, vanilla extract, and egg yolks until well combined. Reduce mixer speed to low and beat in dry ingredients until just combined.

In a clean bowl with clean beaters, beat egg whites until stiff peaks form. Stir 1/3 egg whites into batter to lighten it. Gently fold remaining egg whites into batter just until well combined. Divide batter among ramekins, almost filling them.

Place filled ramekins on a baking sheet and bake for about 25 minutes or until a toothpick inserted into the cake comes out clean. Invert ramekins on a serving platter or individual serving plates and allow them to sit that way, with inverted ramekin still on plate, for at least 10 minutes. Carefully lift off ramekins. Should any pineapple slices stick to the bottom of the ramekin, simply use a blunt knife to life them off and place on top of cake. Serve warm, at room temperature, or cold.

Freezer Friendly!
Freeze cooled leftover cakes wrapped tightly in plastic wrap. When ready to eat, simply bring to room temperature and serve, or if desired, warm for about 20 to 30 seconds in the microwave.

Nutella Swirl Cupcakes

Fans of Nutella, a delicious and versatile cocoa hazelnut spread, will be wild for these cupcakes. They're quick and easy to make and there's no need for frosting as the Nutella, baked into the cake, more than handles the job. While Nutella is the most commonly found brand in the U.S., other brands of cocoa hazelnut spread will also work well in this recipe.

Yield: 12 cupcakes   Serving Size: 1 cupcake

1 3/4 cups flour
2 teaspoons baking powder
1/4 teaspoon salt
1/4 cup neutral canna-oil
1/4 cup canna-butter
3/4 cup sugar
3 large eggs
2 teaspoons vanilla extract
3/4 cup Nutella

Preheat oven to 350 degrees F. Line 12 muffin cups with paper liners. In a medium bowl, stir together flour, baking powder, and salt until well combined. Set aside.

In a large bowl with an electric mixer, beat together cannabis-infused oil and cannabis-infused butter until smooth. Beat in sugar until thoroughly combined and smooth. Beat in eggs, one at a time. Reduce mixer speed to low to stir in the dry ingredient mixture. Increase speed and beat until smooth, about 30 to 40 seconds. Batter will be thick.

Divide the batter among the 12 paper-lined cups. Drop about a tablespoon of Nutella into each cup. To create a marble texture, use a blunt knife to swirl the Nutella through the batter, leaving some exposed on top and burying some within the batter. Bake for about 25 minutes or until a cake tester inserted into the vanilla section of a cupcake comes out clean. Cool slightly before serving.

Freezer Friendly!
Package leftover cupcakes in a plastic freezer storage bag. Bring to room temperature and enjoy.

Red Velvet Cupcakes with Cream Cheese Icing

For some reason, red velvet cake always elicits wows from guests, probably because of its dramatic look, and these cupcakes, kicked up with our extra added ingredient, are no exception.

Yield: 24 cupcakes   Serving Size: 1 cupcake

Cupcakes
2 1/2 cups all-purpose flour
1 1/2 cups sugar
1 teaspoon baking soda
3/4 teaspoon salt
6 tablespoons cocoa powder
1 1/2 cups neutral canna-oil
1 cup buttermilk
2 large eggs

2 tablespoons red food coloring
1 teaspoon distilled white vinegar
1 teaspoon vanilla extract

Icing
8 ounces cream cheese
1/2 cup butter
1 teaspoon vanilla extract
3 1/2 cups confectioners' sugar

Preheat oven to 350 degrees F. Line 24 muffin cups with paper cupcake liners.

In a medium bowl, stir together flour, sugar, baking soda, salt, and cocoa powder. In a large bowl beat together the canna-oil, buttermilk, eggs, food coloring, vinegar, and 1 teaspoon vanilla extract with an electric mixer. Add the dry ingredients and mix just until smooth. Divide batter among prepared muffin cups, filling each about 2/3 full. Bake until a toothpick inserted in the center of a cake comes out clean, about 20 minutes. Cool completely before frosting.

To prepare frosting, beat together cream cheese, butter, and 1 teaspoon vanilla extract with an electric mixer until light and fluffy. Lower mixer speed and slowly beat in confectioners' sugar until incorporated. Increase speed and beat until frosting is light and fluffy. Spread over completely cooled cupcakes, leaving a small rim unfrosted to allow the cake to peak through. If you like the look of the red cake crumbs on top of the icing like in our photo, but don't want to sacrifice a medicated cupcake for the cause, do what I did and purchase a slice of red velvet cake at the bakery to turn into crumbs to sprinkle over the frosted cupcakes.

 Freezer Friendly!
Freeze frosted cupcakes in freezer bags, stacked between layers of waxed paper. Thaw at room temperature or in the refrigerator. Freeze extra icing in lidded containers until the next time you bake.

Old-Fashioned Buttermilk Brownies with Cocoa Frosting

Can't decide if you prefer fudgy or cakey brownies? This recipe makes one that is somewhere in the middle for the best of both worlds. The cocoa frosting takes this treat over the top, but the brownies are plenty good without it.

Yield: 9 brownies   Serving Size: 1 brownie

Brownies
1/2 cup all-purpose flour
1/4 cup unsweetened cocoa powder
1/2 teaspoon salt
1/4 teaspoon baking powder
6 tablespoons canna-butter,
   at room temperature
4 ounces chopped bittersweet chocolate
3/4 cup sugar
2 large eggs
3/4 cup buttermilk
1 teaspoon vanilla extract

Mix-and-Match Add-Ins (Optional)
1 cup chopped nuts, chocolate chips, white
   chocolate chips, cocoa nibs, peanut butter
   chips, raisins, or sweetened dried cranberries

Frosting
4 tablespoons unsalted butter
1/4 cup unsweetened cocoa powder
1/4 cup heavy cream
1 1/2 cups confectioners' sugar

Preheat oven to 350 degree F. Butter an 8-inch square baking pan and lightly dust with flour. In a medium bowl, stir together the flour, cocoa, salt, and baking powder until well combined. Set aside.

Melt the canna-butter and chocolate together in a double boiler set over barely simmering water. Alternately melt canna-butter and chocolate in a glass bowl in the microwave, stopping to stir every 30 seconds. In either case, stir frequently and remove from heat as soon as mixture is smooth. Allow mixture to cool for 10 minutes.

In a large bowl, beat the sugar and eggs with an electric mixer set at medium speed until thick and yellow, about 5 minutes. Lower mixer speed and beat in buttermilk and vanilla, then beat in cooled chocolate mixture. Continue to mix until smooth. Use a wooden spoon or rubber spatula to stir in flour mixture until just combined. Stir in optional add-in ingredients. Pour batter into prepared pan, using the spoon or spatula to smooth top surface and spread batter into the corners. Bake for 15 minutes. Remove pan from oven and rap it 3 or 4 times on a heat-protected surface. Return pan to oven and bake for another 20 minutes or until a cake tester inserted into the cake comes out with just a few moist crumbs attached. Cool completely in pan.

Beat butter with an electric mixer until light and fluffy. Beat in cocoa powder and cream. Slowly beat in confectioners' sugar until mixture is light, fluffy, and all ingredients have been combined. Spread over brownies after they are completely cooled and before cutting.

Freezer Friendly!
Freeze extra frosted brownies in a single layer before wrapping in plastic wrap or foil and storing in a plastic storage bag. Bring to room temperature and enjoy. (These brownies are even good frozen!)

Toffee Chocolate Chip Cookies

Buttery toffee adds an extra dimension to an already great chocolate chip cookie recipe.

Yield: 26 cookies   Serving Size: 1 cookie

1 1/2 cups all-purpose flour
1/2 teaspoon baking soda
1/4 teaspoon baking powder
1 teaspoon salt
6 tablespoons canna-butter
2 1/4 grams kief or finely ground dry hash
3/4 cup firmly packed brown sugar
1/2 cup sugar
1 large egg
1 1/2 teaspoons vanilla extract
1 1/2 cups chocolate chips
3/4 cup toffee chips
3/4 cup chopped walnuts or pecans (optional)

Preheat oven to 350 degrees F. Grease 2 large baking sheets with vegetable shortening, or alternately line them with parchment paper. In a small bowl, mix together flour, baking soda, baking powder, and salt until well combined. Set aside.

With an electric mixer fitted with the paddle attachment, cream together the canna-butter, kief or ground hash, brown sugar, and sugar until well incorporated. Add the egg and vanilla and mix until just combined. Slowly mix in the dry ingredients and stir just until combined. Stir in the chocolate and toffee chips and nuts, if using.

Scoop out about 2 tablespoons dough and press gently to form a flattened cookie. Repeat with remaining dough, placing cookies about 2 inches apart on the prepared baking sheets. Bake for about 15 minutes or until lightly browned. Let set for 5 minutes before transferring to a wire rack to cool completely. Serve warm or at room temperature. Baked cookies will stay fresh for about 4 days in an airtight container.

Freezer Friendly!
Form unbaked dough into cookies. Place on a baking sheet and freeze before transferring to a freezer storage bag. Bake frozen cookies on a greased or parchment-lined sheet at 375 degrees F for about 18 minutes or until browned.

Snickerdoodles

The small Pennsylvania Dutch cookies with the funny name are deceptively simple. It's only cinnamon and sugar that gives them their terrific flavor. Because of this simplicity, I prefer to make this cookie with kief or hash. I find the finished cookie tastes better, as the somewhat nutty flavor of the kief or hash blends better than the more common herbal undertones of cannabis-infused butter.

Yield: 26 cookies   Serving Size: 2 cookies

1 3/4 cups sugar, divided
2 teaspoons cinnamon
1 1/3 cups all-purpose flour
1/2 teaspoon cream of tartar
1/4 teaspoon baking soda
1/4 cup butter, at room temperature
3 grams kief or finely ground dry hash
1 large egg
1 teaspoon vanilla extract

Preheat oven to 375 degrees F. Lightly grease a baking sheet or cover with parchment paper. In a small bowl, stir together 1/4 cup sugar and cinnamon until well combined. Set aside.

In a small bowl, stir together the flour, cream of tartar, and baking soda until well combined. Set aside.

In a large bowl, beat butter and remaining sugar with an electric mixer on high speed until light and fluffy, about 2 minutes. Sprinkle in kief or ground hash and beat until cannabis concentrate is evenly distributed in the butter. Beat in the egg, then beat in the vanilla. Reduce speed to medium-low and gradually mix in the flour mixture just until blended.

Scoop out cookies, about 1 1/2 tablespoons each, and roll between your hands into a semi-flattened ball. Roll in cinnamon-sugar mixture to completely coat the outside and then place on prepared baking sheet about 2 inches apart. Bake for about 10 to 12 minutes or until fairly firm and just beginning to brown. Transfer to wire rack to cool.

 Freezer Friendly!
Freeze unbaked, cinnamon-sugar–coated dough balls in a single layer before transferring to a plastic freezer bag. Bake just the number of frozen cookies you need at 375 degrees F until starting to brown, about 12 to 15 minutes.

Oatmeal Raisin Spice Cookies

Chewy, spicy, and studded with sweet little raisins, these cookies are an old-fashioned favorite.

Yield: 26 cookies   Serving Size: 1 cookie

1 cup all-purpose flour
1/2 teaspoon baking powder
1/2 teaspoon baking soda
1/4 teaspoon salt
2 teaspoon ground cinnamon
3/4 teaspoon ground nutmeg
1/2 teaspoon ground ginger
1/4 teaspoon ground allspice
1 cup canna-butter
3/4 cup packed dark brown sugar
1/4 cup sugar
1 large egg
1 1/2 teaspoons vanilla extract
3/4 cup rolled oats
1 cup raisins

Preheat oven to 350 degrees F. Grease 2 large baking sheets, or alternately line them with parchment paper.

In a medium bowl, combine flour, baking powder, baking soda, salt, cinnamon, nutmeg, ginger, and allspice. Stir to combine. In a large bowl, beat canna-butter with brown sugar and sugar with an electric mixer until well combined and fluffy. Beat in egg and vanilla. Beat in dry ingredients just until combined. Add oats and raisins and beat just until combined. Do not overmix!

Place drops of dough, about 1 3/4 tablespoons each, about 2 inches apart on the prepared baking sheets. Bake for about 15 minutes or until lightly browned. Let stand for 2 minutes before removing to a wire rack to cool.

Freezer Friendly!
Form unbaked dough into cookies and place on a baking sheet. Freeze before transferring to a freezer storage bag. Bake frozen cookies on a greased or parchment-lined sheet at 375 degrees F for about 18 minutes or until browned.

Crispy Rice Treats

Using Crispy Brown Rice Cereal (look for it in health food stores or online), makes this recipe healthier without sacrificing taste. For a less healthy version, substitute chocolate crisp rice cereal for regular, but be warned, the resulting treats are ultra sweet! Whichever way you go, forgoing the traditional brand of crispy rice cereal keeps you from supporting a company who felt the need to promptly fire their popular spokesperson after he was photographed with a bong.

Yield: 1 (8-inch) square pan   Serving Size: 1/9 of pan

2 tablespoons butter
1/2 (7-ounce) jar marshmallow creme
2 1/2 grams kief or finely ground dry hash
3 cups Crispy Brown Rice Cereal
1 cup chocolate chips, white chocolate chips,
    and/or sweetened dried cranberries (optional)

Spray an 8-inch square pan with cooking spray. Butter a spatula. Set aside. Melt butter over low heat in a large saucepan. Add marshmallow creme and stir until completely melted. Stir in hash or kief until dissolved and evenly distributed. Stir in optional ingredients, if using. Remove from heat and quickly stir in cereal until well coated.

Use the buttered spatula to press mixture into prepared pan. Cool. Cut into 9 squares. Best if served the same day.

 Freezer Friendly!
Wrap individual portions tightly in plastic wrap and freeze. Let stand at room temperature for about 15 minutes to thaw and enjoy.

Useful Tools for Cannabis Cooks

If you already cook, you probably have most everything you need to be a cannabis cook. That said, there are a few essential items you should definitely take stock to make sure you have on hand, and a few others that while not absolutely essential, will make life easier. The items below are specific to cannabis cooking.

Scales—If you are dealing with large amounts of plant material (as when making large batches of cannabis butter or oil), a good kitchen scale can help you determine the right amount to use. When cooking with kief or hash, a small jeweler's scale will give you a more accurate gram measurement. While some kitchen scales offer gram measurements, most are not that precise at such small amounts. You can pick up an inexpensive jeweler's scale for about $5.00 (check eBay).

Colander or Large Strainer—Necessary for separating plant material from liquid when infusing butter or oils.

Gravy Separator—This small pitcher with the spout at the bottom makes it easy to separate cannabis-infused oils from the water they were cooked with.

Cheesecloth—Use a double layer of cheesecloth to filter fine particles of plant material from cannabis-infused butter and oil.

Small Coffee or Spice Grinder—A small electric grinder, dedicated to this purpose, is the quickest and easiest way to grind hash. Take care to grind quickly and just until powdered as electric grinders do produce heat.

Ramekins and Other Individual Cookware—Small, inexpensive ceramic ramekins are perfect for making portion-controlled cannabis-infused foods that can go from refrigerator or freezer to oven. Other cookware that makes it easy to make portion-controlled foods include muffin tins, individual pie or tart pans, small loaf pans, and individually sized baking dishes.

Slow Cooker—While you can make cannabis-infused butter or oil on the stovetop, a slow cooker makes the task far easier and less messy. It also helps reduce the strong herbal odor of simmering marijuana.

Gloves—Your hands can get sticky when handling plant material. Disposable latex gloves or even reusable kitchen gloves, while not essential, eliminate the problem.

Rubbing Alcohol—Removes sticky residue from hands, gloves, and kitchen surfaces.

Recipes by Type of Cannabis Used

This handy chart lets you see, at a glance, which recipes in this book are made with cannabis-infused butter, cannabis-infused oil, hash or kief, or ground bud. Technically you can substitute hash or kief in all of the recipes calling for cannabis infused butter or oil, or ground bud. The reverse is not always so. If you have easy, inexpensive access to concentrates, the finished flavor will be less herbal than cooking with butter and oil infusions.

I've grouped all the cannabis-infused oil recipes together even though most will specify either olive oil or neutral-flavored oil. In a pinch, you can substitute one for the other. When a given recipe includes different options for adding cannabis, I've cross-referenced the recipe in multiple categories here.

Recipes Made with Cannabis-Infused Butter

Snacks & Appetizers
Buffalo-Style Hot Wings

Brunch & Lunch
Cranberry Applesauce Bread
Chocolate Chip Banana Bread
Lemon Raspberry Scones
Cinnamon Rolls with Cream Cheese Icing
Eggs Benedict
Southern-Style Shrimp and Grits

Main Courses
New Orleans-Style "Barbecue" Shrimp
Fettuccine Alfredo
Stir-Fried Ginger Shrimp and Asparagus

Sides & Extras
Real Mashed Potatoes
Southern Sweet Potato Casserole
Buttermilk Biscuits
Corn Bread
Garlic Bread Deluxe

Desserts
Key Lime in the Coconut Crust Tartlets
Summer Fruit Cobbler
Hot Fudge Dessert Sauce
Molten Chocolate Lava Cakes
Mini Pineapple Upside-Down Cakes
Old-Fashioned Buttermilk Brownies with
    Cocoa Frosting
Toffee Chocolate Chip Cookies
Oatmeal Raisin Spice Cookies

Recipes Made with Cannabis-Infused Oil

Snacks & Appetizers
Asian Shrimp Salad Rolls

Soups
Gazpacho

Salads & Salad Dressings
Almost Caesar Salad
Summer Grilled Corn Salad
Grilled Vegetable Quinoa Salad
Tabouli
Italian-Style Tuna and White Bean Salad
Classic Italian Vinaigrette
Asian-Style Vinaigrette
Honey Mustard Dressing

Brunch & Lunch
Carrot Bran Muffins
Asian-Style Steak Salad
Easy 5-Minute Medicated Pizza Dough
Easy Pizza Sauce
New Orleans-Style Muffuletta Sandwiches

Main Courses
Pesto Sauce

Sides & Extras
French-Style Roasted Potatoes
Garlic Bread Deluxe

Desserts
Lemon Berry Swirl Cheesecake Tarts
Carrot Cake Cupcakes with
    Cream Cheese Icing
Nutella Swirl Cupcakes
Red Velvet Cupcakes with
    Cream Cheese Icing

Recipes Made with Ground Bud

Snacks & Appetizers
Shrimp and Pork Potstickers
Mini Meatballs in Chile Sauce

Soups
Albondigas (Mexican Meatball Stew)

Main Courses
Vegetable Lasagna
Better-Than-Mom's Meatloaf
Medicated Meatballs in Marinara

Recipes Made with Kief or Hash

Snacks & Appetizers
Guacamole Deluxe
Sun-Dried Tomato Tapenade
Black Olive Tapenade
Hot Artichoke Dip
Hummus
Shrimp Rémoulade
Steamed Artichoke with Garlic Aïoli
Deviled Eggs
Bacon-Wrapped Stuffed Figs
Roast Beef Roll-Ups
Mini Curry Samosas
Crab Rangoon
Shrimp and Pork Potstickers
Mini Meatballs in Chile Sauce
Gougères
Argentine-Style Empanadas
Sliders

Soups
Chilled Cucumber Avocado Soup
Curried Carrot Soup
Roasted Garlic and Onion Soup
French Onion Soup au Gratin
Cream of Butternut Squash Soup
Scottish Cock-A-Leekie Soup
Albondigas (Mexican Meatball Stew)

Salads & Salad Dressings
Fruit Salad-Stuffed Cantaloupe
Wedge Salad with Blue Cheese Dressing
Cucumber and Sweet Onion Salad
Creamy Coleslaw
Asian-Style Slaw
Best-Ever Potato Salad
Buttermilk Ranch Dressing
Thousand Island Salad Dressing

Brunch & Lunch

Chocolate Chip Banana Bread
Mini Ham and Cheese Quiches
Eggs Benedict
Over-Stuffed Twice-Baked Potatoes
The Ultimate Tuna Sandwich or Salad
Chicken and Cashew Sandwich or Salad
Easy Anytime Medicated Quesadilla
Bean and Cheese Burritos
Stuffed Open-Face Sandwich Melts

Main Courses

Chiles Rellenos
Lobster Newburg
Chicken or Tofu Green Chile Enchiladas
Chicken Curry
Chicken Pot Pies with Puff Pastry Crust
Cornish Game Hens with Peach, Sausage,
    and Rice Stuffing
Beef Stroganoff
Better-Than-Mom's Meatloaf
Medicated Meatballs in Marinara
Apple and Cornbread-Stuffed Pork Chops
Barbecue Sauce for Meats

Sides & Extras

Cauliflower Gratin
Real Mashed Potatoes
Steakhouse-Style Creamed Spinach
Corn Pudding
Lemon Risotto with Asparagus
Mushroom Risotto
Macaroni and Cheese for Grown-Ups
Herbed Yeast Dinner Rolls

Drinks

Mango Lassi
Devilishly Good Orange Smoothie
Peaches and Cream Smoothie
Piña Colada Smoothie
Strawberry Licuado
New York-Style Chocolate Egg Cream
Iced Café Latte
Hot Café Mocha
Triple-Chocolate Hot Chocolate
Masala Chai Tea
Thai-Style Iced Tea
Thai-Style Iced Coffee

Desserts

Chocolate Peanut Butter Tarts
French Vanilla Ice Cream
Butterscotch Dessert Sauce
Dark Chocolate Truffles
Carrot Cake Cupcakes with
    Cream Cheese Icing
Snickerdoodles
Crispy Rice Treats

Worthwhile Marijuana Organizations and Educational Resources

It does my heart good to know that so many dedicated individuals and organizations are working tirelessly to reform our nation's, and for that matter the world's, harmful marijuana laws. All of the following national organizations bring value to the movement in my opinion. They each have a different focus and a slightly different agenda, but all are working to make things better for marijuana patients and the public at large.

If you find you do not agree with the marijuana laws you are subjected to, it's time to exercise your rights and work to change them. These organizations can help you make that change happen.

This list is by no means complete. In addition to these big national organizations, there are many small local chapters and nonprofit groups working to make change happen. You can usually find those in the calendar sections of many of the Web sites below.

NORML (National Organization for the Reform of Marijuana Laws)—A public-interest lobby that for more than 30 years has provided a voice for those Americans who oppose marijuana prohibition. NORML represents the interests of the tens of millions of Americans who smoke marijuana responsibly and believe the recreational and medicinal use of marijuana should no longer be a crime. In addition to national NORML, there are numerous individual local chapters and the NORML Women's Alliance that provide a chance for citizens all over the country to get active in effecting change. **www.norml.org**

LEAP (Law Enforcement Against Prohibition)—LEAP seeks to reduce the multitude of unintended harmful consequences resulting from fighting the war on drugs and to lessen the incidence of death, disease, crime, and addiction by ending drug prohibition. LEAP's goals are: (1) To educate the public, the media, and policymakers about the failure of current drug policy by presenting a true picture of the history, causes, and effects of drug use and the elevated crime rates more properly related to drug prohibition than to drug pharmacology, and (2) To restore the public's respect for police, which has been greatly diminished by law enforcement's involvement in imposing drug prohibition. While much of LEAP's membership is composed of current and former law enforcement officials, this not a requirement to join or support this fine organization. **www.leap.org**

SSDP (Students for Sensible Drug Policy)—SSDP is an international grassroots network of students who are concerned about the impact drug abuse has on our communities, but who also know that the War on Drugs is failing our generation and our society. SSDP mobilizes and empowers young people to participate in the political process, pushing for sensible policies to achieve a safer and more just future, while fighting back against counterproductive Drug War policies, particularly those that directly harm students and youth. While SSDP's focus is on youth, you don't need to be young or a student to support this worthy group of activists. **www.ssdp.org**

ASA (Americans for Safe Access)—ASA's mission is to ensure safe and legal access to cannabis (marijuana) for therapeutic uses and research. The focus of ASA is strictly medical marijuana and not overall legalization. **www.safeaccessnow.org**

MPP (Marijuana Policy Project)—MPP and the MPP Foundation envision a nation where marijuana is legally regulated similarly to alcohol, marijuana education is honest and realistic, and treatment for problem marijuana users is non-coercive and geared toward reducing harm. Their mission is fourfold: to increase public support for non-punitive, non-coercive marijuana policies; to identify and activate supporters of non-punitive, non-coercive marijuana policies; to change state laws to reduce or eliminate penalties for the medical and non-medical use of marijuana; and to gain influence in Congress. **www.mpp.org**

DPA (Drug Policy Alliance)—DPA envisions a just society in which the use and regulation of drugs are grounded in science, compassion, health, and human rights; in which people are no longer punished for what they put into their own bodies but only for crimes committed against others; and in which the fears, prejudices, and punitive prohibitions of today are no more. Their mission is to advance those policies and attitudes that best reduce the harms of both drug use and drug prohibition and to promote the sovereignty of individuals over their minds and bodies. **www.drugpolicy.org**

The Human Solution—While still a small Southern California grassroots organization, this group is gaining steam and expanding into new territories. This is largely due to the popularity of their Solidarity Ribbons (like the one I am wearing in the photos on the cover of this book), which are fast becoming a symbol for the medical marijuana movement. The tasteful green ribbons adorned with small medical-style crosses make an easy way to show support and solidarity in courtrooms, at rallies, or anytime you want to start a conversation about medical cannabis. The Human Solution's mission is to provide education and support to medical marijuana patients, providers, and the community at large by attending court hearings, speaking publicly at city council and town hall meetings, giving classes to educate the public and remove the stigma of medical marijuana, and holding fund-raising events to help with defendants' legal expenses and assist patients in need. The Human Solution's core belief, like mine, is that nobody should EVER go to jail over a plant. **www.the-human-solution.org**

Index

About the Author: Cheri Sicard

Cheri Sicard was a professional food writer and recipe developer before she became a medical marijuana patient and cannabis cook. She created the popular cooking Web site FabulousFoods.com and is the author of *The Complete Idiot's Guide to Easy Freezer Meals* (2011, Alpha Books), and the editor of the freezer and make-ahead cooking blog CheriOnIce.com. When writing this book, she approached cannabis recipe development from the perspective of being a foodie, believing there's no reason to have to choke down bad-tasting or boring edibles in order to receive the benefits of edible marijuana.

Had someone told Cheri back in 1996, when California's Prop 215 first legalized marijuana for medicinal use, that she would become entrenched in the cannabis movement, she wouldn't have believed them. Other than the rare toke at a party, Cheri didn't use marijuana. It wasn't until she was nearly 40 years old that her doctor suggested, off the record as the hospital he worked for didn't "allow" it, she try marijuana to help with a chronic nausea problem that a variety of prescription drugs had failed to help. It worked immediately. After regularly using cannabis for a while, Cheri was surprised to discover she no longer felt the need for the anti-depressant prescriptions she'd been taking for years, as for her, cannabis did the job better without unwanted side effects. Lifelong chronic digestive problems disappeared, too.

While Cheri marveled at how cannabis had improved the quality of her daily life, she worried that she might somehow be doing herself harm. Like most Americans, she had been indoctrinated into the school of thought that marijuana is an evil and dangerous drug. So, she started reading books and doing research on the internet. She even went so far as to attend and graduate from Oaksterdam University, the cannabis industry's leading training institution. Afterward, she continued to attend classes and seminars at every opportunity.

The more Cheri learned, the more the scientific evidence bowled her over and convinced her that the marijuana she was using improved not only specific symptoms, but overall health and well-being as well. She found it impossible to keep quiet about all the astounding medical research that's routinely ignored by the mainstream media and started talking about it to everyone she knew. She continually found herself outraged by government hypocrisy surrounding the war on drugs and the fact that people all over the county, including in states where the people have voted to make medical marijuana legal, are still being jailed over this benevolent plant.

Over the course of six months Cheri went from the typical closeted American marijuana user to an outspoken cannabis legalization and anti-drug war advocate. And she hasn't looked back since. When she isn't cooking and developing new recipes, you can often find Cheri speaking at civic meetings and city and county councils, organizing rallies, teaching classes, and attending court supports for medical marijuana defendants.

Through it all, she is always working side-by-side with other medical marijuana patients. Many are people like her, who have realized a dramatic improvement in the quality of their day-to-day lives by using cannabis. Others with serious and life threatening conditions like AIDS, cancer, PTSD, multiple sclerosis, Crohn's disease, and countless other debilitating ailments, could not bear to live without the relief cannabis gives them. The valuable input, opinions, and support of all these people has lead Cheri to start work on Volume II of *The Cannabis Gourmet Cookbook: Quick and Easy Cooking with Marijuana.* Look for it soon from your favorite bookseller or online at www.CannabisCheri.com.